ATD Soft Skills Series

T0284710

Emotional Intelligence
in Talent Development

Patrick Malone

PRESS

Alexandria, VA

ATD Press is an internationally renowned source of insightful and practical information on talent development, training, and professional development.

ATD Press
1640 King Street
Alexandria, VA 22314 USA

Ordering information: Books published by ATD Press can be purchased by visiting ATD's website at td.org/books or by calling 800.628.2783 or 703.683.8100.

Library of Congress Control Number: 2021939768

ISBN-10: 1-952157-49-8
ISBN-13: 978-1-952157-49-3
e-ISBN: 978-1-952157-50-9

ATD Press Editorial Staff
Director: Sarah Halgas
Manager: Melissa Jones
Community of Practice Manager, Career Development: Lisa Spinelli
Developmental Editor: Jack Harlow
Production Editor: Hannah Sternberg
Text Design: Shirley E.M. Raybuck
Cover Design: John R. Anderson Jr.

Printed by BR Printers, San Jose, CA

Contents

About the Series v

Series Foreword vii

Introduction xiii

Part 1. The Case for Emotional Intelligence

    Chapter 1. The Power of Emotional Intelligence 3

    Chapter 2. Why Emotional Intelligence Matters 13

    Chapter 3. The Bumpy Road to Emotional Intelligence 21

Part 2. Emotional Intelligence and Talent Development

    Chapter 4. The Role of the Talent Development Professional 35

    Chapter 5. Stress 43

    Chapter 6. Multitasking 61

    Chapter 7. Communication 75

    Chapter 8. Conflict 89

    Chapter 9. Where to Go From Here 103

References 111

Index 115

About the Author 123

About the Series

The world of work is changing. As companies once prioritized radical workplace performance and productivity improvements, they focused on training their employees with the purpose of getting more work done faster. But companies have learned that while their people might be increasingly productive, they aren't working better, particularly with each other. Lurking on the horizon is always greater automation, which will continue to shift the balance between the needs for hard and soft skills. Employees of the future will spend more time on activities that machines are less capable of, such as managing people, applying expertise, and communicating with others. More than ever, soft skills are being recognized as a premium.

Enter talent development.

TD professionals play a unique role in addressing the increasing demand for soft skills. They work with people and on behalf of people: A trainer facilitating a group of learners. A team of instructional designers working cross-functionally to address a business need. A learning manager using influence to make the case for increased budget or resources. But how can TD professionals expect to develop future employees in these soft skills if they're not developing their own?

At the Association for Talent Development (ATD), we're dedicated to creating a world that works better and empowering TD professionals like you to develop talent in the workplace. As part of this effort, ATD developed the Talent Development Capability Model, a framework to guide the TD profession in what practitioners need to know and do to develop themselves, others, and their organizations. While soft skills appear most prominently under the Building Personal Capability domain, these crucial skills cross every capability in the model, including those under Developing Professional Capability and Impacting Organizational Capability. Soft skills enable TD professionals to take their instructional design, training delivery and facilitation, future readiness, change management, and other TD capabilities to the next level.

Just as TD professionals need resources on how to develop talent, they need guidance in improving their interpersonal and intrapersonal skills— to be more adaptable, self-aware and empathetic, creative, team-oriented and collaborative, and influential and persuasive. This ATD series provides such guidance.

Organized with two parts, each book in the ATD Soft Skills Series tackles one soft skill that TD professionals need to foster in themselves to help the people and organizations they serve. Part 1 breaks down the skill into what it is, why it's important, and the internal or external barriers to improving it. Part 2 turns the lens on the daily work of TD professionals and how they can practice and perfect that skill on the job. Featuring worksheets, self-reflection exercises, and best practices, these books will empower TD professionals to build career resiliency by matching their technical expertise with newfound soft skill abilities.

Books in the series:
- *Adaptability in Talent Development*
- *Emotional Intelligence in Talent Development*
- *Creativity in Talent Development*
- *Teamwork in Talent Development*
- *Influence in Talent Development*

We're happy to bring you the ATD Soft Skills Series and hope these books support you in your future learning and development.

Jack Harlow, Series Editor
Senior Developmental Editor, ATD Press

Series Foreword

Oh, Those Misnamed Soft Skills!

For years organizations have ignored soft skills and emphasized technical skills, often underestimating the value of working as a team, communicating effectively, using problem solving skills, and managing conflict. New managers have failed because their promotions are often based on technical qualifications rather than the soft skills that foster relationships and encourage teamwork. Trainers as recently as a dozen years ago were reluctant to say that they facilitated soft skills training. Why?

Soft Skills: The Past and Now

The reluctance to admit to delivering (or requiring) soft skills often starts with the unfortunate name, "soft," which causes people to view them as less valuable than "hard" skills such as accounting or engineering. The name suggests they are easy to master or too squishy to prioritize developing. On both counts that's wrong. They aren't. In fact, Seth Godin calls them "real" skills, as in, "Real because they work, because they're at the heart of what we need today" (Godin 2017).

Yet, as a society, we seem to value technical skills over interpersonal skills. We tend to admire the scientists who discovered the vaccine for COVID-19 over leaders who used their communication skills to engage the workforce when they were quarantined at home. We easily admit to not knowing how to fly an airplane but readily believe we are creative or can adapt on the fly. We think that because we've been listening all our lives, we are proficient at it—when we're not. As a result, we put much more emphasis on developing our technical skills through advanced degrees and post–higher education training or certifications to land that first or next job than we do on mastering our interpersonal and intrapersonal skills.

Fortunately, many businesses and their leaders are now recognizing the value of having a workforce that has technical knowledge supported by soft skills. That's good because soft skills matter more to your career than you may envision. Consider: as a part of the Jobs Reset Summit, the World Economic Forum determined that 50 percent of the workforce needed reskilling and upskilling. The summit also identified the top 10 job reskilling needs for the future. Eight of the 10 required skills in the 21st century are nontechnical; these skills include creativity, originality, and initiative; leadership and social influence; and resilience, stress tolerance, and flexibility (Whiting 2020). LinkedIn's 2019 *Global Talent Trends Report* showed that acquiring soft skills is the most important trend fueling the future of the workplace: 91 percent of the respondents said that soft skills matter as much or more than technical skills and 80 percent believed they were critical to organizational success (Chandler 2019). A Deloitte report (2017) suggested that "soft skill–intensive occupations will account for two-thirds of all jobs by 2030" and that employees who practice skills associated with collaboration, teamwork, and innovation may be worth $2,000 more per year to businesses. As the cost of robots decreases and AI improves, soft skills like teamwork, problem solving, creativity, and influence will become more important.

Soft skills may not be as optional as one might originally imagine.

Soft Skills: Their Importance

Soft skills are sometimes referred to as enterprise skills or employability skills. Despite their bad rap, they are particularly valuable because they are transferable between jobs, careers, departments, and even industries, unlike hard or technical skills, which are usually relevant only to specific jobs. Communication often lands at the top of the soft skill list, but the category encompasses other skills, such as those included in the ATD Soft Skills Series: emotional intelligence, adaptability, teamwork, creativity, and influence. These personal attributes influence how well employees build trust, establish accountability, and demonstrate professional ethics.

Soft skills are also important because almost every job requires employees to interact with others. Organizations require a workforce that has technical skills and formal qualifications for each job; however, the truth is that business is about relationships. And, organizations depend on relationships to be successful. This is where successful employees, productive organizations, and soft skills collide.

Soft Skills and the Talent Development Capability Model

Talent development professionals are essential links to ensure that organizations have all the technical and soft skills that are required for success. I sometimes get exhausted just thinking about everything we need to know to ensure success for our organizations, customers, leaders, learners, and ourselves. The TD profession is no cookie-cutter job. Every day is different; every design is different; every delivery is different; and every participant is different. We are lucky to have these differences because these broad requirements challenge us to grow and develop.

As TD professionals, we've always known that soft skills are critical for the workforce we're responsible for training and developing. But what about yourself as a TD professional? What soft skills do you require to be effective and successful in your career? Have you ever thought about all the skills in which you need to be proficient?

ATD's Talent Development Capability Model helps you define what technical skills you need to improve, but you need to look beyond the short capability statements to understand the soft skills required to support each (you can find the complete model on page 37). Let's examine a few examples where soft skills are required in each of the domains.

- **Building Personal Capability** is dedicated to soft skills, although all soft skills may not be called out. It's clear that communication, emotional intelligence, decision making, collaboration, cultural awareness, ethical behavior, and lifelong learning are soft skills.

Project management may be more technical, but you can't have a successful project without great communication and teamwork.

- **Developing Professional Capability** requires soft skills throughout. Could instructional design, delivery, and facilitation exist without creativity? You can't coach or attend to career development without paying attention to emotional intelligence (EI) and influence. Even technology application and knowledge management require TD professionals to be adaptable, creative, and team players for success.

- **Impacting Organizational Capability** focuses on the soft skills you'll use while working at the leadership and organizational level. For you to have business insight, be a partner with management, and develop organizational culture, you will need to build teamwork with the C-suite, practice influencing, and use your EI skills to communicate with them. Working on a talent strategy will require adaptability and influence. And you can't have successful change without excellent communication, EI, and teamwork. Future readiness is going to require creativity and innovation.

Simply put, soft skills are the attributes that enable TD professionals to interact effectively with others to achieve the 23 capabilities that span the spectrum of disciplines in the Capability Model.

Soft Skills: The Key to Professionalism

So, as TD professionals we need to be proficient in almost all soft skills to fulfill the most basic responsibilities of the job. However, there's something even more foundational to the importance of developing our soft skills: Only once we've mastered these skills can we project the professionalism that will garner respect from our stakeholders, our learners, and our peers. We must be *professional,* or why else are we called *TD professionals?*

Professionalism is the driving force to advance our careers. To earn the title of TD professional we need to be high performers and exhibit the qualities and skills that go beyond the list of technical TD skills. We need to be soft-skill proficient to deliver services with aplomb. We need to be team members to demonstrate we work well with others. We need to be EI-fluent to ensure that we are aware of, control, and express our emotions and handle interpersonal relationships well. We need to be creative to help our organization achieve a competitive advantage. We need to be adaptable to future-proof our organizations. And we need influencing skills that help us earn that proverbial seat at the table.

We all need role-specific knowledge and skills to perform our jobs, but those who achieve the most are also proficient in soft skills. You will use these skills every day of your life, in just about every interaction you have with others. Soft skills allow you to demonstrate flexibility, resourcefulness, and resilience—and as a result, enhance your professionalism and ensure career success. And a lack of them may just limit your career potential.

Clearly, soft skills are more critical than once thought and for TD professionals and trainers they are likely to be even more critical. Your participants and customers expect you to be on the leading edge of most topics that you deliver. And they also expect you to model the skills required for a successful career. So, which soft skills do you need to become a *professional* TD professional? Is it clearer communication? Interpersonal savvy? Increased flexibility? Self-management? Professional presence? Resourcefulness?

E.E. Cummings said, "It takes courage to grow up and become who you really are." I hope that you have the courage to determine which skills you need to improve to be the best trainer you can be—and especially to identify those misnamed soft skills that aren't *soft* at all. Then establish standards for yourself that are high enough to keep you on your training toes. The five books in the ATD Soft Skills Series offer you a great place to start.

Elaine Biech, Author
Skills for Career Success: Maximizing Your Potential at Work

Introduction

Saia had done all the right things.
She'd gone to college, built an extensive résumé, and amassed an even more impressive array of skills. In fact, Saia had a long and successful track record of talent development and acquisition since joining the company several years ago. It seemed she had an almost otherworldly ability to identify potential in young professionals.

When the firm decided to promote Saia, it was a big deal. Now she was in charge of the Talent Acquisition Division, overseeing a staff of 14 with complete responsibility for the strategic direction of the division.

Right away she gathered her new team together to share her views on how their work should be done: In short, do it just like she did it. And why not? She was successful, and had recently been promoted. She knew best, right? And, it was in this very first meeting that the wheels began to fall off.

While Saia excelled in the operational proficiency necessary for her work, that didn't help in how she related to those around her. As a newly minted supervisor, she struggled to transition her technical talent to supervisory expertise. And when it came to her own self-awareness and regulation, she was far less prepared, and fell short at monitoring her own nonverbal cues. She often lost her temper when others couldn't understand her approach and struggled to handle the conflict that ensued. She was brilliant, but scattered. Her assistant, Hakeem, couldn't keep her on task. Every time he broached the topic with Saia, it ended badly. Everyone was frustrated and Saia was losing her patience.

Something was missing.

That something is emotional intelligence.

Stories like Saia's are all too common in the workplace, across all functions and hierarchies. It's because we put far too much stock in credentials. There, I said it! It's not an abnormal thing when you think about it. We need those pesky acronyms attached to our titles, we really do, along with all of the training, certification, and degrees that come with them. They are essential for the work we do. They allow us to build our technical skills. They also give us the street cred to land our first job. In some cases, they even help us advance in our career.

But as with Saia, less thought is often put into how we are developing our emotional intelligence skills throughout our career.

Why Do We Overlook Emotional Intelligence?

For many years, good people, committed, diligent, and intelligent, have created reports by surveying what the experts say is necessary for effective management and leadership. Many of these studies are released each year with press releases and much fanfare.

It's only natural that organizations respond to them. They build leadership development and succession plans based on the advice. They hire the experts to guide them in leading in today's (fill-in-the-blank) world. The proposed schematics seemingly represent an easy fix to the host of problems that organizations face. It's much easier to depend on attractive frameworks with charts, figures, and diagrams than to do the hard work of developing environments of trust and innovation where people are enthused and motivated. Thus, we fall victim to tactics like becoming strategic instead of developing the competencies we require to connect with, and lead, others. What tends to be missing in these approaches is all tied to emotional intelligence: the bridges to others built on compassion, forgiveness, caring, empathy, kindness, and love.

Confession time: I love the topic of emotional intelligence. Am I a tree-hugger? Yep. Eternal optimist? You bet. Barry Manilow fan? Oh yeah. Here comes Mr. Positive again; everyone hold hands! I'm used to it. I've spent the majority of my career in leadership positions and made all the mistakes that one could possibly make. If there's one thing I have learned over the years, it's that it is not about what you know; it's about who you are. For a large portion of my career, I was a uniformed naval officer. I've lost count of the number of people who came to me and said, "It must've been easy to lead as a naval officer; all you have to do is give orders." Nothing could be further from the truth. Ordering people to do work is coercion, pure and simple. I firmly believe that the most effective leaders derive success not from their positional authority, but from their willingness to serve and care for others.

The program that I direct at American University, the Key Executive Leadership Programs, has been around for almost 50 years. From the beginning, we have been focused strongly on kindness, emotional intelligence, gratitude, mindfulness, compassion, increasing thinking capacity, journaling, and meditation. I love to remind people that we came into being only a couple of years after The Beatles released *Let It Be*. This album, and much of their music, was about love. Our founder, Don Zauderer, a dear friend and mentor of mine, had a vision for the Key program that was also based on love. Of course, the content is there: best practices, case studies, rigorous academic research, and writing. But what matters the most, in my view, are the concepts that Don stressed so much for his entire career: how we build trust with others, how we care for one another, how we treat one another, and how we bond. Knowing who you are, and being comfortable with that, allows you to connect authentically with others. Everything else flows from there.

And here's what I believe: Connecting at the human level is where leadership begins and ends, whether you've got leader in your title or you're a line employee trying to advance your organization. We're all leaders, no matter the position we hold. There is no stronger force than the human heart and soul. Bond with another and you have a committed teammate, employee, or boss for the rest of eternity. Everyone is healthier. The culture is happier. The organization excels. Those are the facts—scientifically based (which we'll get into) and irrefutable.

Now, back to Saia. Once promoted, she likely read those leadership reports. She had a good heart, and certainly had the intellectual capacity for the technical aspects of her job. And although that story was framed in the context of a promotion, emotional intelligence is not only a factor once we are promoted. It's always a factor. Emotional intelligence governs all our interactions with human beings. This may be when we're a part of a team, working for someone, working with someone, or overseeing those who work for us. As long as humans are involved, emotional intelligence will matter. Saia needed some work here.

How This Book Will Help You

For talent development professionals, emotional intelligence is especially crucial. Keep in mind that to work in human development, which is what talent development truly is, you must have people skills. Granted, you will be required to have a strong palette of technical qualifications. Employers are looking for people who are strong analysts, comfortable with the minute details of instructional design, skilled at building and tracking recruiting models, and astute at managing complex projects. These proficiencies matter, and they can be taught to anyone with the aptitude for such material. But on their own, they are inadequate for the complex world faced by talent development professionals today. Human developers must first and foremost have strong people skills, and those pesky soft skills, which don't come easy, are required for building teams, managing conflict, communicating, influencing, ensuring trust, and meeting organizational objectives.

That's what this book is about: emotional intelligence, the emotional cousin of the intelligence quotient. It is a foundation we use to come in contact with our soft skills, and a tool to build those competencies as talent development professionals. When the competencies are used properly, the result is better self-awareness, a better ability to read and motivate others, and a better sense of life balance.

We'll cover a lot in the next 100 pages or so. In part 1, we'll walk through what emotional intelligence is and how it relates to what we normally view as human intelligence. We'll explore the five dimensions of emotional intelligence: self-awareness, self-regulation, motivation, empathy, and social skills. Mindfulness will also be an important topic of exploration as we grapple with the mindset necessary for gaining comfort with the unknown, mastering resilience, and practicing self-care—the last of which we often ignore. We'll also examine why emotional intelligence matters to the self, to organizations, and to our business, along with the barriers we face when attempting to grow into these competencies.

Part 2 speaks directly to the talent development profession and how emotional intelligence can be used in conjunction with the various roles we play in developing others, especially with regards to building personal, professional, and organizational capability. And because we know how busy those who grow others can be, we'll confront the emotional, physical, and performance-related effects of stress, along with our propensity to multitask our way out of it. For better or worse, we all do it.

Got conflict? Of course we do. Show me the workload of a lead instructional designer, a learning development specialist, or a vice president of training and development, as they navigate external stakeholders, subject matter experts, and busy adult learners, and I'll show you conflict. And finally, we have to delve into communication. It is the vehicle through which we share our emotional intelligence with others. Sometimes communication is verbal, other times not, but it's always there, and it sends very, very, very strong messages whether we acknowledge it or not.

Getting in the Emotional Intelligence Frame of Mind

Are you up for this? I can't wait. As a talent development professional, you have a unique role in the organizations of today. In fact, unique may not be strong enough. Think critical. You are the mechanism by which companies harness the most valuable resource they have—the human being.

As we wind our way down this path over the next nine chapters, you will be doing as much thinking and writing as you are reading.

Throughout the book, I will ask you to stop and think, and I hope you do. This will allow the material to sink in and give you a chance to jot down a few notes about how you are feeling or questions you have. Put the book away for a few minutes and let your mind wander. I believe this is a much more effective approach than the traditional academic focus on Likert scale questions and numerical assessments, many of which are arbitrary and have little scientific basis.

This book is about you, and it depends on you, so you'll have to work for this one! Open-ended, thought-provoking questions, combined with mindfulness and journaling, will embed the key concepts of emotional intelligence in your mind and practice.

Along those lines, let's start with this quick exercise. Examine the following table, which lists different types of emotions.

Happiness	Sadness	Anger	Contentment
Anticipation	Disappointment	Confusion	Desire
Anxiety	Interest	Distress	Awkwardness
Disgust	Calmness	Craving	Awe
Joy	Jealousy	Sympathy	Nostalgia
Empathy	Love	Fear	Contempt

Now answer the following three questions. Don't think too hard. Your gut response will be the best one.

1. Which of these emotions describes where you spend the majority of your time?

_____

_____

2. Which of these emotions do you fear the most?

_____

_____

3. Which of these emotions do you wish you could feel more?

_____

_____

Let's get rolling!

PART 1

The Case for Emotional Intelligence

CHAPTER 1

The Power of Emotional Intelligence

Initial Thoughts

Over many years of working with people who are interested in improving their professional skill sets and advancing in their careers, I have noticed one thing that is the most common denominator of their professional makeup, and I am guilty of it as well. We are proud of what we know. We tend to rely so heavily on the expertise we gain as part of our professions that we ignore the importance of so-called soft skills.

This is unfortunate because it is not so much what we know that will drive success in our work and in our lives, but how we make other people feel. Maya Angelou, the late poet and author, said this much more eloquently than I just did: "People will forget what you said, people will forget what you did, but people will never forget how you made them feel." How we make people feel matters. It matters more than anything. When people feel they can trust us, when they feel empathy from us, and when they can sense our authenticity, they are far more likely to be partners with us in whatever endeavors we choose to undertake. Emotional intelligence (EI) gets us there. It empowers us with everything we need to connect and communicate with others. The benefits are extraordinary.

A Brief History of EI

The idea of emotional intelligence has grown in popularity over the years, and thank goodness it has. Many will credit the more recent, and popular, leadership researchers for the work behind emotional intelligence but it began much longer ago than many think. Consider the turn of the 20th century in the United States. Having built on the Industrial Revolution some 50 years before, American factories were up and running in a big way. While this meant plenty of work for the citizenry, the environment was far from ideal. Intimidating bosses wandered factory floors in workshops that were often unsafe and dangerous, to say the least.

It was this very type of leader, and the failings of their controlling style, whom early humanists sought to warn about. Loud voices, overt supervision, and little tolerance may have been the order of the day, but critics recognized that there should be more to the workplace. In the early 1900s, a social worker and consultant named Mary Parker Follett, often referred to as the "Mother of Modern Management," made tremendous inroads supporting the concept of working through others to achieve an organizational mission. Other like-minded folks agreed, and a slew of studies extolled the ideas of social intelligence, affective intelligence, and a more humanistic approach. Maslow's hierarchy is a living relic from these days, along with other studies supporting the idea of emotional strength and self-awareness.

Most agree that the term emotional intelligence first appeared in a doctoral dissertation by Wayne Payne in 1985. This was followed by the groundbreaking article "Emotional Intelligence," in the journal *Imagination, Cognition and Personality*, by psychologists Peter Salovey and John Mayer, who are often credited as the founders of emotional intelligence. Other voices such as Travis Bradberry, Jean Graves, Sivan Raz, Leehu Zysberg, and Daniel Goleman followed with exceptional works on emotional intelligence and its practical application in the workplace.

Emotional Intelligence Defined

Perhaps the best way to think about emotional intelligence is by considering your own experience. Reflect for a moment upon a time when you worked for someone who, let's say, wasn't someone you would consider one of your better bosses! Perhaps it wasn't as bad as the turn-of-the-century factory conditions I just described, but it wasn't great. Now, jot down a few adjectives describing the boss in question.

_____

_____

Got it? Now, think about someone you worked for to whom you would give your discretionary energy. In other words, you were willing to go above and beyond in thought and deed for this person. Now, write down a few words to describe that individual:

_____

_____

Let me guess, a few of the words you probably wrote in your second list include: inspiring, unpretentious, caring, good listener, sensitive, empathetic, compassionate, humble, good communicator, kind, self-effacing, encouraging. How close was I?

Your second list contains the prime indicators of what emotional intelligence actually is. Emotional intelligence connotes one's ability to be in touch with their feelings, regulate their actions, recognize those needs in others, and manage relationships accordingly. People who are intellectually astute and technically competent may or may not be emotionally intelligent; we'll get to that later. But those who are emotionally intelligent excel at building connections with others. They have that vibe about them that makes them approachable, no matter the position they hold. And they're able to build workplaces of trust, communication, and inspiration.

Emotional intelligence is not as complex as you may think, but it is involved. It requires us to take a deep dive into our own selves and see a picture that is not always pretty. From that point forward, we are positioned for more impactful relationships in and outside the workplace. And it's deceptively simple! According to Goleman (1998), one of the more prominent voices in the field, emotional intelligence can be seen as falling into five basic domains: self-awareness, self-regulation, motivation, empathy, and social skills. Each one opens the door to a better understanding of ourselves and others.

Self-Awareness

Ever take a long look at yourself in the mirror and see yourself as you are? Not as others see you, or as you wish for them to see you. Have you ever recognized something in your behavior or language that surprised you? Perhaps someone else brought it to your attention and you thought, "Wow, I really am that way!"

There is no emotional intelligence without self-awareness. Self-awareness allows us to recognize the emotions we experience. It also allows us to see ourselves for who we are: the good, and the not so good. When we look in the mirror, we cannot hide. The same goes for self-awareness. By becoming more attuned to our inner signals and embracing them for what they are, we build an inner confidence that forms the foundation for our emotional intelligence. We know what motivates us. We are better able to moderate our responses to others, be sensitive to their emotions, and communicate more thoughtfully and clearly.

Consider for example an instructor who lacks self-awareness. Chris may have all of the latest content and best practices at the ready, but he is unaware that the language he uses in the classroom causes distress and anxiety among a handful of learners. He is also woefully unaware that he tends to speak only to the left side of the room. It is a simple and unintentional gesture, but it makes the rest of the class feel uncomfortable and left out. When a student approaches him about this, he immediately becomes defensive.

People who get high marks in self-awareness bring a lot to the table. They recognize their emotions and are better able to understand the impact those emotions have on their performance. Knowing that they have a paralyzing shyness about presenting in front of a group may spark them to spend more time in preparation, for example. Sometimes this knowledge manifests as an inner signal—that pesky messenger that reminds us of the true self within. Those with strong self-awareness are attuned to this signal, and they embrace it.

Because high self-awareness individuals are able to zero in on signs within, they often excel at self-assessment. They know their strengths and play to them well. However, they also know their weaknesses, and work in a humble and curious way to strategically position themselves around others who have the requisite talent. And, they welcome feedback from those around them, whether it be colleagues, direct reports, or bosses. It's the knowledge that's key, and self-aware individuals understand the long-term value of that knowledge. They know their strong points, and they know when to ask for help.

I've spent a lot of time on self-awareness because it is the most important dimension of emotional intelligence. Researchers have found a significant connection between self-awareness and our ability to succeed in some of the other important dimensions of emotional intelligence. For example, when we demonstrate self-awareness, we have a 50 percent chance of exhibiting sound self-regulation and a 38 percent chance of demonstrating social awareness skills such as empathy. Not too bad. But without self-awareness, we have virtually zero chance of self-regulation and are 83 percent more likely to lack social awareness skills (Boyatzis and Burckle 1999).

Self-Regulation

What drives you nuts? Seriously. Think about it. Is it when someone doesn't look you in the eye when they speak? Or people who roll through four-way stop signs? What about people who are rude to servers in a restaurant? That bubbling anger or frustration you feel is real. But what do you do about it? What actions do you take, or not?

The emotions we recognize when we are self-aware are amazingly powerful. They can position us to make well-thought-out, pragmatic decisions, or they can launch us down a path of behavior that we regret when we wake up the next morning.

Take for example the possibility of two managers faced with a resource dilemma. Kiandra has an incoming staff of 12 and has been told she must give up some of her new team to Angela. Angela is hoping for a 50–50 split, gaining six new people. Kiandra decides to share only two of the 12, keeping 10 for herself. Angela gets angry and tells Kiandra to forget the whole thing.

Angela gets a failing grade in self-regulation. Instead of getting two new people for her team, she was so flustered that she ended up with no one. This denotes a classic inability to self-regulate. Her emotions overwhelmed her decision-making ability to the point that she actually hurt her team.

Stephen Covey (2020) refers to this phenomenon as response-ability—the ability to choose our response to any situation. It has also been termed the "amygdala hijack," or the brain's response to an emotional threat (Goleman 1995). Such a failure to self-regulate is all too common and, while good in emergencies, may rob us of our ability to make sensible decisions in normal times.

Motivation

What gets you up in the morning? Is it a desire to make a difference in the world, or do something in tune with your values? Where does your passion lie? How do you infuse that passion in your day-to-day life?

Motivation plays a critical role in emotional intelligence because it is the way we harness our incentives for achievement. We all have the desire to accomplish something, such as being the best instructional designer or talent specialist. But those goals are met through a blend of intrinsic or extrinsic drives, the former being the desire that comes from within, and the latter being those more external goals, such as money or time off work. Neither is bad when balanced with a healthy approach toward professional goals.

Motivation is exceptionally important when times are difficult. Take as an example a situation in which an instructional designer, Eniko, is struggling to work with a new supervisor. Even though it may be difficult, she stays focused on the purpose of the work she does, and the value it creates in the classroom. This awareness of what motivates her intrinsically can carry her through any number of workplace challenges, even a bad supervisor!

Emotionally intelligent individuals show motivation through initiative, commitment, and positivity. They are self-starters who need little prodding to kick off a new project or undertake a challenging task. They persevere when times are tough, demonstrating a resilient nature that stays strong despite setbacks. Finally, they are optimists, finding the positive in situations where others may not.

Empathy

Are you able to recognize when someone else is in need? Do you have radar for sensing that something may be awry in a situation and the ability to offer comfort to others—comfort that brings both of you to tears?

Empathy means feeling what others feel, to the degree that you can. Empathy is a unique component of emotional intelligence in that it requires us not only to embrace the emotions we feel, sometimes even from years past, but also to sense and respond to the emotions of others. It begins with being an attentive listener, something extremely rare in a world full of distractions. By truly listening, we are able to tap into the true message of the speaker. This sets the stage for a connection that is uniquely human.

The need for empathy in the world of instruction is not unusual. Let's say that a facilitator, Shabbar, is attempting to instruct a group of learners on a very complex topic. One of the learners, Susan, approaches Shabbar at the break to inform him that she has an anxiety disorder that causes her to lose focus when she is in a room with a large number of people. Susan is embarrassed and is looking for an empathetic and supportive response. Shabbar responds with a gentle and kind manner that puts her at ease.

We often find it difficult to exhibit empathy, along with other aspects of emotional intelligence (see chapter 3). One reason is we confuse empathy and sympathy. Sympathy tends to come from a hypercritical place, in which we assess the other person's situation and render a judgment. It's not a particularly supportive approach. Empathy, conversely, brings us closer to one another. Empathetic people are attuned to the signals others send, whether they be verbal or nonverbal. They are then able, via sensitive and deliberate actions, to reach out, support, and bond through shared emotions.

Social Skills

If someone were watching you walk down the hall, around the office, or to your car, what would they witness? Would they see conversation and engagement with others? How do you interact with people from different backgrounds?

Social skills, sometimes referred to as relationship management, are the outward manifestation of all the emotional intelligence dimensions. It's what people see, whether it be the dynamics with a boss, a teammate, or maintenance staff. Social skills play an important role in emotional intelligence because they encompass an individual's ability to be self-aware, regulate their behavior, stay motivated, and be empathetic.

In the classroom example with Shabbar, consider what would happen if Susan were to exhibit outward signs of discomfort or tension while the class is in session. If Shabbar were to respond in an empathetic and caring way—for example, if he were to stop the instruction as long as it takes to make her feel comfortable and get everything back on track—the class would witnesses his ability to be effective at relationship management. However, if he were to respond with an annoyed glance and an insensitive tone, he would fail the social skills test.

Team members in the workplace recognize strong social skills in individuals who work well with people from other departments, or up and down the hierarchy. These people are equally comfortable with the most senior leadership, the most junior interns, and across generations. They are excellent communicators, whether in person, through email, or in print. They have a strong rapport and recognized character, and are well liked.

IQ, EQ, My Q, Your Q

Now that we've covered the dimensions of emotional intelligence, we should touch on its counterpart, the intelligence quotient (IQ). So, which is better? Your emotional intelligence, measured as your EQ, or your IQ? To make a direct comparison between these two constructs, it is probably best to make sure we understand exactly what an intelligence quotient truly is.

Many of us have taken an IQ test. You might've taken one when you were busy searching the internet for a great salsa recipe and stumbled upon an offer to get your IQ in five minutes with a quick online test. Answer a few logical-reasoning questions, maybe uncover a missing number in a sequence, and do a little algebra, and you can find out where you fall on the intellectual spectrum.

The earliest attempts to measure intelligence were completed by Paul Broca (1824–1880) and Sir Francis Galton (1822–1911), who argued they could measure intellect by measuring the size of the human skull. (Hmm, I think we'll pass on that one.) Later attempts to assess intellect included the Simon-Binet IQ test in 1904; designed for children, it formed the basis for the more modern approaches. Since then, IQ testing has been conducted in various forms for everything from school admissions to job screening to sociocultural research—even, sometimes, for nefarious purposes. And despite the fact that scientists still debate the use of IQ tests, we find ourselves attracted to them, just like salsa.

To distinguish between IQ and EQ, we can return to the teachings of our friend Dan Goleman. He describes IQ as the intellectual capability necessary to master the threshold competencies of a given field of expertise. Think of it as cognitive capacity. And of all the cognitive abilities out there, only one, pattern recognition, was associated with outstanding leaders. Between 90 and 95 percent of the difference between an average leader and an outstanding leader was due primarily to the level of their emotional intelligence (Goleman, Boyatzis, and McKee 2013). And Alfred Binet, of the Simon-Binet test, eventually viewed IQ tests as a faulty way to measure intellect because they were missing ways to measure emotional intelligence.

From a management and leadership perspective, the answer to the question, "Which one is better, IQ or EQ?" is not that difficult. Although IQ may offer clues as to our ability to master a body of knowledge, it does little for our ability to lead and work with others. EQ, conversely, is about our ability to connect with and inspire others. It's just that simple.

 Consider This
- Have you ever leaned on your expertise instead of your interpersonal skills?
- Did it make you more comfortable?
- How do you feel about feelings?

Wrap-Up

Sounds pretty good, doesn't it? In truth, the concepts of emotional intelligence are not terribly complicated. That is one of the beauties of our exploration. It actually makes a lot of sense when you think about it. If you want to connect with others, build relationships, and be sensitive to yourself and what you bring to the table, emotional intelligence is crucial. But there are a whole host of other reasons you should jump on the emotional intelligence train. Read on!

CHAPTER 2

Why Emotional Intelligence Matters

Feeling Good. Is It Enough?

OK, let me guess what you're thinking. Emotional intelligence—self-awareness, self-regulation, motivation, empathy, and social skills—sounds terrific on the surface. It makes us feel good and gives us hope in humanity. It is a positive force that links people together and bonds us in ways that nothing else can. The impact of emotional intelligence on our human self, our teams, and our organizations is much more significant than you might initially think. And the better news? The practices and techniques we use to master emotional intelligence are very simple.

In this chapter, let's review the case for emotional intelligence for both ourselves and our organizations. And in explaining its importance, we'll also touch on the need for mindfulness and self-care.

The Case for Emotional Intelligence: Benefits to Self

George had a complete lack of self-awareness about how he interacted with other members of the instructional team. He was not aware that he often interrupted during team meetings. People could barely get a word out before George would correct them and direct the conversation elsewhere. He wasn't doing this to be rude; he was just an energetic and driven team member. After Michelle reached out to George to share with him his tendency for cutting other people off, he was completely embarrassed. He simply was not aware that this was something that he had been doing.

Becoming aware of his behavior, unintentional though it was, was a huge step in building his relationship with the rest of the team.

The benefits of emotional intelligence for ourselves are immense. Think for a moment about what emotional intelligence comprises. First, ability to be self-aware: to understand and recognize your emotions as they arise, followed immediately by a talent for regulating words and actions resulting from those emotional signals. Couple this with a deep understanding of your motivation, an empathetic approach to others, and the ability to manage yourself socially, and it would be difficult to argue that the word immense is an overstatement. Emotional intelligence can truly transform an individual.

First and foremost, emotional intelligence leads to better human relationships. Research has shown that individuals with high levels of emotional intelligence enjoy much healthier interpersonal relationships both in and out of the workplace (Six Seconds 2018). They are more readily able to foster relationships of trust, compassion, love, and connection with others, building the human bond that we all desire, whether we admit it or not. They are also less prone to depression (Goleman 2004).

These people enjoy physical health benefits as well, and who doesn't want that? Strong EQ has the capacity to reduce stress levels. Indeed, the ability to recognize and manage emotions positions you to recognize the impact of stress before it takes a negative toll on your body, lessening the impact of resultant conditions such as arthritis and diabetes, and limiting the impact of hypertension (Bar-On 2006).

Finally, perhaps one of the most impactful benefits of strong emotional health is resilience. In challenging times, people with emotional intelligence find it easier to cope with change and adversity. They are emotionally in tune with themselves and are not easily overwhelmed by negativity. Their ability to center themselves allows them to absorb the impact of unexpected challenges, difficult though they may be. This transcends into better decision making, which leads to better performance, individually and organizationally.

Consider This

- Have you ever found that you were completely unaware of a practice, bias, or feeling that you carry?
- How did you feel after this was brought to your attention?
- What actions did you take?

The Case for Emotional Intelligence: Benefits to the Organization

Significant change was long overdue for a training institute located in the upper Midwest. The previous leadership had created an environment of distrust and toxicity. Senior supervisors often interrupted classroom instruction and directed designers to create lesson plans that were quite outdated and often ineffective. Morale was bad, until a new dean joined the organization. Judette not only engendered a sense of calm and professionalism in the organization, but she also brought her own team of senior educational administrators, all of whom were extremely well-versed in the competencies of emotional intelligence.

Before long, their behaviors and values filtered down through the organization, and what had been a place on the brink of disaster became one of the most sought-after places to work in the industry. Individuals collaborated across divisions to create exciting new programs marked by innovation and exceptional delivery. Cross-functional teams worked well together and trust ran rampant. It was a good place to be.

It may be long overdue, but the field of organizational science has finally recognized the impact of emotional intelligence. For too many years, leadership experts have focused on best practices and strategic whatevers to fashion our perspective on leadership, when the answer has always been directly in front of us, or more specifically, inside of us. And the impact on our organizations is significant.

To begin, those skilled in the competencies of emotional intelligence are better communicators with those they lead or interact with. They are able to connect at a more human level, which enhances the possibility of trust. They are also able to communicate better with those they work for because they are able to read their bosses to ascertain where their focus may be. A more complete understanding of the motivations of those around us, whether they work for us or we work for them, increases clear messaging and decreases misunderstandings in day-to-day operations. And as for learners? Understanding and bonding with them ensures an organization's viability, pure and simple.

There are other advantages as well. Because they understand their own motivations and what drives them, those with strong emotional intelligence perform better than their colleagues. Their inner sense of direction is robust, and they are able to engage more readily with the tasks they face. And because emotional intelligence transcends professions, they tend to advance more quickly in their careers regardless of the type of work they do. Because they communicate with others well, they tend to be better problem solvers.

Finally, in addition to performing better, emotionally intelligent workforces are happier. A happy, centered workforce is likely to lead to efficient and effective practice. Workplace conflict is kept to a minimum, and when it does occur, it is handled in a professional, caring manner. The workforce is also less likely to suffer from job burnout and tends to use fewer sick days. Their organizations can expect less turnover, which directly affects human resource costs and drives results.

> ### ☀️ Consider This
> - Have you ever worked in an organization where people did not get along and trust was a rarity?
> - How did you feel about getting up and going to work each day?
> - Did you have any physical or emotional reactions?

The bottom line is always the bottom line, as they say, and little goes as far as emotional intelligence in securing successful organizational performance. Whether it be communication and understanding of clients, or the work of teams, or charting the future of the organization, nothing goes further than emotional intelligence toward achieving an organization's mission. And better yet, it costs nothing! Being an empathetic listener, being patient, thinking before speaking, and being self-aware have no expenses. They require only our attention.

The Mindfulness Connection

Mindfulness is a 2,500-year-old practice that has its roots in the Eastern world. In fact, mindfulness is mentioned in the ancient text *Satipatthana Sutta*, which translates to "The Discourse on the Establishing of Mindfulness." In this historic writing, the Buddha describes mindfulness as a focus on the body (including the breath), sensations or feelings, the mind/consciousness, and thoughts. Those who practice mindfulness strive to be fully present and become more aware of who they are, including how they are feeling mentally and physically. They seek to be nonjudgmental and thoughtful, in balance with the life that surrounds them.

The link to emotional intelligence is quite direct. Emotional intelligence provides the building blocks to a more mindful life. When we are self-aware, we recognize and embrace our emotions. When we exhibit self-regulation, we harness the impulses we feel to make rash decisions, send nasty emails, or speak unkindly. When we understand what motivates us at the deepest levels, we are able to find our true vocation in life, one to which we can devote our heart and soul. When we show empathy to others, we sit in a nonjudgmental posture that bonds us closer together. And when we exhibit these competencies through our visible social skills, we are more aware of the bigger picture and how we fit in.

🔆 Consider This

- How do you center yourself?
- Is this something that you do often?
- How do you feel when you are unable to engage in this practice?

A Word About Self-Care

It may seem odd that when talking about emotional intelligence, we have such a strong focus on self. Strong emotional intelligence competencies give us the ability to connect with others, bond, trust, and feel. Emotional intelligence truly is a pathway to giving, being a steward, and walking humbly. So it's strange that the fuel for this passage is self. Work on self, listen to self, meditate with self, and regulate self. Sounds sort of selfish doesn't it? It's not.

Consider the words of Parker Palmer (1999) in his book *Let Your Life Speak*:

> **Self-care is never a selfish act—it is simply good stewardship of the only gift I have, the gift I was put on earth to offer others. Anytime we can listen to true self and give the care it requires, we do it not only for ourselves, but for the many others whose lives we touch.**

Palmer penned these words more than 20 years ago and they still ring true. So much in our lives draws us away from simple self-care. We work endless hours in demanding jobs. We struggle with relationships in and out of the workplace. And social media demands that we have our best face on at any given time. There just never seems to be enough time in the day.

Self-care not an easy path upon which to embark. When we make time for ourselves, we are by definition taking time away from others. We may feel guilt or overcompensate by trying to work harder or longer to make up for our "selfish" time. Of course, this is exactly the wrong choice. The fact is that when we make time for self, even just a little, we come out stronger and better than ever. Our relationships improve, we're more productive, and we're healthier. It's the right thing to do for ourselves and others.

Consider This

- Do you practice any form of self-care?
- If not, what are the barriers that contribute to you being unable to care for yourself?
- If you had absolutely nothing to do tomorrow morning, how would you spend your time?

Wrap-Up

Organizationally, personally, and professionally, emotional intelligence has the capacity to make significant improvements in the way we deliver training and development to all our learners. But, truth be told, it is not an easy road. There are several bumps and bruises to be had on the way to effective implementation of emotional intelligence, regardless of the individual or organization. Read on!

CHAPTER 3

The Bumpy Road to Emotional Intelligence

If It Matters So Much, Why Don't We Just Do It?

Everything about emotional intelligence makes sense in terms of its application and benefits. However, the road to building emotional intelligence is fraught with hinderances and inhibitors. Many things can get in the way. They may be internal factors, including barriers or fears we may or may not be aware of. In any case, they can be formidable blockades to EQ. Let's run through four commons barriers.

The Adult Mind

This is a tricky place to start. Our own mind blocks us? Our mind is the genesis of everything that we say and do, so we might come to the conclusion that because the mind is a barrier, we can never achieve emotional well-being. This is not true, but it is important to understand the stages of our mind so that we are able to better position ourselves for the pursuit of strong emotional health.

Simply stated, we see the world the way we are. We as human beings view our surroundings and the people around us through the lens of our own biases and filters. This is not necessarily a bad thing, unless we don't recognize it and fail to take the time to learn enough about the way that we think in order to address it. (Remember self-awareness?) On top of that, the way we see the world changes over time. As we grow, as our life experiences shape who we are, and as conditions change, our views change too.

Research by Robert Kegan and Lisa Lahey (2017) has provided a solid foundation for understanding the complex workings of the human mind. It's important to know that we all move through distinctive, progressive phases of meaning-making ability as we grow. Each phase is more complex than the previous. As we reach the latter stages of mind, we shed the preprogrammed, defensive self, and become more adaptable, tolerant, and inclusive.

In their simplest terms, these stages progress from the socialized mind to the self-authoring mind to the self-transforming mind.

The Socialized Mind

People who possess the socialized stage of mind find great comfort in the approval of those around them. They are fashioned by the expectations of the individuals, practices, and professional identities of those they wish to identify with the most.

For example, Kyla is a curriculum development expert working in an organization that preaches the "process model." She has always been happy to go with the flow and design her curriculum as the organization prefers, even though she suspects that there may be a better approach out there somewhere. She is not one to rock the boat. She much prefers the approval of those around her.

The Self-Authoring Mind

In the self-authoring mind construct, people demonstrate an ability to assert their own belief system or set of values—even if it falls outside the normal perspective accepted by the masses. This is not necessarily a combative stance, it's simply a different way of seeing things that is supported by the individual's self-esteem.

Kyla eventually develops the confidence to offer a new perspective on the curriculum design process in her organization. This is a risky endeavor. By discovering her ability to step forward and argue for a different approach to curriculum design, she is showing signs of the self-authoring mind.

The Self-Transforming Mind

People with a self-transforming mind do not feel the urgency to make a decision quickly; rather, they are at ease embracing diametrically opposed perspectives and exploring potential solutions. This mind set is able to view challenges in a broader systematic or cultural way.

Kyla has expanded her search for different approaches to curriculum. She has discovered so many innovative options she finds appealing that she has now entered the world of comfort with the unknown. She is looking at her work through a broader systems perspective, weighing the impact of her design with factors beyond the classroom.

■　■　■

So why does it matter whether we have a socialized mind, self-authoring mind, or self-transforming mind? Because it allows us to see where we are and open the door to understanding the pathways to where we want to be. None of the aforementioned stages are inherently bad. They simply have their own set of proclivities and boundaries. By gaining an appreciation of how we view the world and how we view ourselves, we are then able to take another step toward stronger emotional intelligence.

Our Thinking Patterns

We have a tendency in the way we think to view the world via the realm in which we find the most comfort. This is due in large measure to the neural pathways the brain uses to function efficiently (Kahneman 2011). When we have a thought or a practice that we are comfortable with, the brain files it away as a go-to, and we thus revert to that thought or practice often. The brain loves this because it's fast and easy. While this may be an advantage during emergencies, it doesn't easily support new thought patterns.

We take extraordinary comfort in these patterns of horizontal thinking, thanks to our instinctive human compulsion for constancy and predictability. We like to know where we've been, where we're going, and what's likely to happen. Even those who present themselves as crazy and unpredictable have measures of expectedness in their lives. But these patterns also support our ability to maintain a stable sense of self, and this is important. We like knowing where we fit in, and we love it when our thoughts are validated. When we're able to be in a place we recognize, enhanced by familiar sights, sounds, and experiences, life is good.

We can see these thinking tendencies in the workplace when we depend on our past practices to confirm our value. Note that I said *depend*. Our previous ways of doing things are not always bad. In fact, they're very important. They signal professional growth and development, advancement in the organization, and our individual mastery in an area of expertise; they also build self-confidence. The old ways may provide a noticeable measure of job satisfaction for the individual.

Despite the coziness offered by this horizontal mindset, there are downsides. Blindly accepting comfort levels, limiting ourselves to only what is visibly measurable, and hiding behind pre-established rituals put us at extreme risk for missing the big picture. Metrics become our savior and routine becomes our diet. We get too task focused and lose the broader systems perspective that is often required for work in the talent development field.

When we remain in this comfort zone, we may be content with goals that stretch us but seldom challenge us to any significant degree. And this is precisely what emotional intelligence requires, a significant challenge to the way we think. Engaging in any type of emotional intelligence growth or development requires that we step outside our comfort zone and think more adaptively. Credentials may get us in the door, but they won't connect us with those we work with or lead.

Fear

What are you most afraid of?

Fear is not necessarily a bad thing. It can keep us safe in the most dire of situations. It can also provide a measure of caution prior to making a difficult decision or executing a new program initiative. Fear can range from something as simple as a fear of spiders to a fear of bridges, medical procedures, or certain situations like public speaking. Everyone has a fear of something!

Each year, Chapman University releases the "Survey of American Fears," and the list is long. Guns, natural disasters, terrorism, government, illness—there's no doubt we live in a culture of fear. Researchers note that when we are afraid, our ability to make decisions and maintain healthy levels of physical and mental fitness is impaired (Bader et al. 2020). Fear can devastate us physically by damaging our immune, digestive, and cardiovascular systems. It can freeze us mentally, diminishing our ability to think clearly and assess the situation. And these conditions can even exacerbate pre-existing ones.

Fear also creates a barrier to our pursuit of emotional intelligence. We might fear straying too far from our recognized scope of expertise on our path to growing the competencies of emotional intelligence. Part of the reason may be due to our natural survival instinct. It's always a risk to try something new, especially in the workplace. We never know exactly how things are going to turn out, so we shy away from attempting something as vulnerable as an emotionally strong connection with our colleagues.

Another key contributing factor to fear is the fear of not knowing. So many of us were taught from an early age that having the answer is the way to succeed, so not knowing makes us uncomfortable. We feel pressure to know all the answers. This is fine until it's not. In 1900, many scientists insisted that mental illness was caused by demons. For years, we thought cholesterol was a deadly killer, but that is debatable today. Just because we think we know the answer does not mean it is correct! And this drive to always know can make us afraid to ask for help.

The fear of not knowing everything can set the stage for leadership challenges at all levels. If bosses wield the "I already know" mentality, their emotional intelligence competencies are probably lacking. Having all the answers leaves little space for good listening or engagement with others and their views.

This was well documented in 1817 by the English Romantic poet John Keats, who pondered the ability to be comfortable while in doubt. He argued that it was difficult for us to sit in uncertainty or mystery. Keats was onto something; when we are comfortable with the unknown, we reach out to others for dialogue, engagement, and comfort. When we are able to escape our inclination to protect our fragile egos and prove to others how good we are, we position ourselves well for growth in our emotional intelligence.

Organizations, Briefly

Organizations have been the focus of tons of research over the years on everything from culture and trust to productivity and development. I would be remiss if I did not make a couple comments about the impact that organizations can have on emotional intelligence, good and bad.

Let's start with what organizations truly are. We often think of them like a chart: lots of boxes and lines connecting people in reporting relationships. There's a lot of structure and a lot of process. There is no escaping the formality that this concept presents—the problem is this view is not completely accurate.

A much better depiction of an organization would be a human cell. Let's return for a moment to high-school biology. A human cell has this really cool, sophisticated balance of chemical relationships among its components. This gentle interplay of the cell allows it to grow, thrive, and protect itself. Mitochondria, lysosomes, endoplasmic reticulum: They all interconnect and depend on one another, just like the people who make up an organization. Organizations are systems that have interrelated subsystems. Let's face it, lines and boxes don't tell the story. Hearts and souls do.

Because an organization is made up of human beings, who have a wide range of emotions, it makes sense that we should be concerned about its emotional intelligence capacity. Is it a place that fosters connection and bonding among its employees? Or is it an environment where distrust and politics rule?

In the least desirable of circumstances, organizations can be significant barriers to the growth of emotional intelligence. Toxic behavior on the part of leaders, or acceptance of the same, blocks any desire to foster an environment where self-awareness, self-regulation, motivation, empathy, and social skills can grow. The resulting organizational culture becomes one of distrust and fear. Innovation is hampered, productivity drops, and sick days and turnover rates increase. The bottom-line bottoms out.

Organizations such as these also struggle to change, which is especially harrowing. Change is hard enough for any company. Any business is in a consistent state of change, demanding more from its employees at every turn. When faced with the need for change, organizations typically move slowly, with the requisite fear and trepidation. The structural inertia in place in most organizations, along with threats to expertise or existing power structures, makes change difficult. But when an organization is also overshadowed by a noxious culture, one bereft of emotional intelligence among leadership, it can find itself in a cycle from which escape is a challenge at best.

Conversely, in the most desirable of circumstances, organizations can serve as veritable petri dishes of development. (Yes, another biology reference!) In an organization marked by strong emotional intelligence, trust is prevalent. And because trust is the lubricant of any well-functioning organization, it follows that the organization will be one of creativity, innovation, and productivity. In a climate of trust, staff members feel safe to be vulnerable and ask penetrating questions. None of this is possible without the presence of the components of emotional intelligence.

Finally, organizations in their most positive form also yield an energy that is almost palpable. It is a synergistic connection of the hearts and souls of those who populate the organization. Some call it organizational culture; others call it organizational climate. Regardless of the name, organizations marked by these positive forces, which are fueled by emotional intelligence, have a competitive edge and true staying power.

The Path to Emotional Intelligence

Emotional intelligence and its related dimensions are a powerful combination for anyone seeking to build a sense of presence and balance in their life. Through disciplined practice, the skills necessary to move toward such goals are easy to learn and simple to repeat. It just takes commitment, an open heart, and an open mind. In light of the barriers we just discussed, I want to offer a few basic actions you can take to overcome them on the road to emotional intelligence.

Embrace the soft side. This is perhaps one of the most difficult tasks you can undertake in developing emotional intelligence. The fact is we have an enduring comfort with data and models. Fancy charts and complex equations validate our way of thinking and "prove" that we're right—except when we're not. While quantitative statistics impress us, they seldom tell the whole story. Metrics do matter. But for every metric produced, there is a person behind that data point, a person with hopes, dreams, needs, and fears. Bond with the person, not the data.

Comfort thyself with the unknown. Sometimes the answers we seek, or even the questions we ask, fall into the category of the unknown. This is not an easy thing for the human brain to accept. Sitting in a state of not knowing often brings physical and mental stress, which makes us edgy and uncomfortable. As I mentioned before, we are neurologically wired for a desire for certainty. It's a survival thing. But being comfortable in the unknown allows us to take a deep breath (literally), sit back, and ask questions. It gives us a welcome respite from the demands of knowing all the answers. It gives us space for thought and, well, space.

Be vulnerable. This is almost as difficult as embracing the unknown, and maybe more so. Being vulnerable requires us to remove the mask we wear—the mask of the talent development executive, the instructor, the coach, the manager. When done well, and with authentic self-awareness, it frees us and allows us to exhibit humility. Vulnerable leaders are seekers, and they need not rely on their professional persona and all the accoutrements of their title to be taken seriously. Empathy, a key emotional intelligence competency, comes easy for the vulnerable because of their willingness to be who they are.

Master resilience. Being resilient is one of the most misunderstood concepts in the workplace. When we think of resilience, we most commonly think of unleashing the robust side of ourselves. When the going gets tough, the tough get going. We pull ourselves up from the doldrums and we try again. Maybe we try to do more with less. We multitask more, stay up later, or work harder. But resilience is actually something quite different: It's all about recovery. It's about taking the time to step back and care for yourself, to heal. It entails a sense of inner peace that soothes the mind and soul.

Meditate. This doesn't have to be as difficult as you might think. Meditation can provide the break we need to find the self-awareness that is so crucial to our emotional and physical health. You don't need pillows, blankets, or candles, although those things are nice! Meditative thought can occur while working in the garden, going to the gym, commuting, or sitting at your favorite coffee shop. But if you really want to delve into meditation in its purest sense, first find a quiet place. Sit or lie down, making yourself as comfortable as possible. Close your eyes and let your mind do its magic. Listen to your body and the sounds around you. You'll be amazed at what you learn.

Journal. That's the verb *journal*, not the noun. Putting pen to paper or fingers to keyboard is an effective way for growing your emotional intelligence. You don't have to write lengthy paragraphs in a leather-bound book. Anything will work. One effective technique to connect with your feelings is to make a list of the roles you play in life: mother, brother, project manager, volunteer, painter. Next to each role, write the first feeling that comes to mind when you think of yourself in that role. By naming that feeling, you place yourself in control, which allows you to select an appropriate response to the feeling rather than just reacting to it.

Reflect on your crucibles. When we think of the word crucible, we often think of those fireproof ceramic bowls from high-school chemistry that withstand extreme temperatures and never break. In a way, that's what our personal crucibles are. Author Warren Bennis (2004) suggested that our personal crucibles are those moments in life when we are truly tested, or when our character is forged by a difficult time. These events challenge our beliefs and values and mold who we are. Reflecting on these crucibles connects us to our past and helps us understand where we are in the present.

Step back from technology. Oh, the horror! You might have to put down your smartphone. Technology has proved to be a double-edged sword—we're super connected, but we're super connected. We get a lot done, but we spend a lot of time getting it done. Try inserting a few blocks of time into each day that are tech-free. While doing so, listen to what's around you. Become an observer of humanity and see what you learn.

Assume noble intent. Let me rephrase that: Assume noble intent in yourself and others. A lovely positivity stems from giving yourself the benefit of the doubt. Not only does it provide physical benefits, but it also keeps you from spinning out of control with doomsday fears (Mayo Clinic Staff 2020). People who stay positive feel better about themselves and others. They are more likely to be creative, innovative, and fun. And don't forget, positivity begets positivity. Not only will you feel good, but those around you will as well.

Keep learning. Nothing is better for the emotional and intellectual brain than a hunger for knowledge. It is far too easy, given the hectic pace of day-to-day life, to fall into routines that have little variety and too much predictability. Try something new each day. Learn a new word. Take a new path while out on a walk. Work on a crossword puzzle. Each time we expose ourselves to something new, we create new pathways of thought and open the mind to endless possibilities.

Wrap-Up

There are multiple facets to the world of emotional intelligence. While it is relatively simple in its conceptual framework, emotional intelligence offers extraordinary benefits to organizations and individuals. The road may be filled with unbelievers primarily because of the comfort zones they have established, but it is a road worth taking. Emotional intelligence plays a unique role in the work of talent development professionals and equips all of us for the practical challenges that we face in the workplace. In part 2, we'll explore those challenges and the ways you can develop your own emotional intelligence skills.

PART 2

Emotional Intelligence and Talent Development

CHAPTER 4

The Role of the Talent Development Professional

People at the Heart

Emotional intelligence is about people. So is the talent development profession. If you don't train people, you work with people on curriculum. Maybe you recruit people, or coach, or work with subject matter experts to design instructional modules. Perhaps you oversee a team of instructional system specialists or you support learners through the registration and administration of post-course evaluations. In the first three chapters of the book, we saw many examples of talent development professionals, the work they do, and the link to the various aspects of emotional intelligence.

The competencies of emotional intelligence, in fact the entire model itself, could be viewed as personal. It almost feels a little selfish spending so much time inside our own heads, addressing our own motivations and emotions. We may journal, meditate, or just sit and ponder. But while this may seem completely self-focused, it is quite the opposite. So, while the emotional intelligence framework can be perceived as individual in nature, it not only benefits our own peace of mind, but bonds us better with others.

We all depend on both ourselves and others to do be able to do our work. And in today's fast-changing world, it is simply hard to go it alone. Extreme change is the norm in the talent development universe. We must stay motivated and self-aware, but we must also harness the minds and commitment of those around us to be successful in our goals. We depend on teams to create exciting new content, assess results, and formulate a strategy. We break people into teams during our training sessions and conferences for the purpose of garnering the best ideas and generating robust discussion. All of this depends on others.

There is one very simple way to think about this. Without people, there is no one to train and no one to develop. This means that for talent development professionals to succeed, they must not only be technical experts in their craft and certified to deliver their work, but also be comfortable with all aspects of working with people. The single best tool for their success is emotional intelligence.

Walking the Talk

As professionals in the world of talent development, we have a responsibility to those we work with and to those we serve to be role models for the people we try to help. Using our methodological expertise and our emotional intelligence competencies, we must strive to "walk the talk." If we are teaching a module on project management, for example, it is imperative that we have an applied understanding of what it means to work around and with other people. If we are designing a teaching plan, we must strive to put ourselves in the shoes of the instructor and the learner, which helps us envision a better picture of the ultimate value of the product we are creating. All of this takes emotional intelligence.

Emotional intelligence positions us for success in the talent development universe. It allows us to strengthen our ability to be aware, both personally and culturally. Our ethical decision-making lenses are clearer, and our ability to work with others is enhanced. We become stronger standard-bearers for the organizations we serve, with newfound insights into how to strategically address issues of volatility, uncertainty, change, and ambiguity in our work. Finally, with sound emotional intelligence competencies, we hone our professional capabilities to their sharpest edges, ensuring success for ourselves and our learners.

Emotional intelligence shows up in all facets of talent development work and in the knowledge and skills those professionals need to develop themselves, others, and their organizations. We can point to the Talent Development Capability Model as evidence (Figure 4-1).

Figure 4-1. The Talent Development Capability Model

Building Personal Capability	Developing Professional Capability	Impacting Organizational Capability
• Communication • Emotional Intelligence & Decision Making • Collaboration & Leadership • Cultural Awareness & Inclusion • Project Management • Compliance & Ethical Behavior • Lifelong Learning	• Learning Sciences • Instructional Design • Training Delivery & Facilitation • Technology Application • Knowledge Management • Career & Leadership Development • Coaching • Evaluating Impact	• Business Insight • Consulting & Business Partnering • Organization Development & Culture • Talent Strategy & Management • Performance Improvement • Change Management • Data & Analytics • Future Readiness

Under the Building Personal Capability domain, emotional intelligence itself shows up as the emotional intelligence and decision-making capability. But as we'll discuss in chapter 8, effective communication requires emotional intelligence to connect with people; express your thoughts, feelings, and ideas; and listen actively to those of others. Collaborating and leading also have an emotional intelligence component with building and managing teams, navigating conflict (chapter 7), and providing feedback. Today's global business climate means that cultural awareness and the ability to foster an inclusive work environment are imperative, and emotional intelligence can help you adapt and adjust your attitude and behavior in diverse situations; having empathy also broadens your viewpoints and encourages cultural sensitivity.

Emotional intelligence underpins the Developing Professional Capability and Impacting Organizational Capability domains, too. Your instructional design needs to reflect empathy for your learners and how they learn best. To deliver and facilitate training, you must be able to self-regulate your emotions and reactions during live sessions and empathize with learners. When coaching others, you need emotional intelligence to establish an environment of mutual respect and trust. To be an effective consultant and business partner, you have to work with other organizational units or departments and manage stakeholders, which requires self-awareness of how you're translating talent development needs into business needs. Managing change requires managing your emotions and others' and dealing with any conflict that arises.

> ### 🔆 Consider This
> - Reflect on your professional life for a moment. What aspects could you improve through emotional intelligence?
> - Reflect on your personal life for a moment. What aspects could you improve through emotional intelligence?
> - What do you consider your most robust emotional intelligence strengths?

Before we get into applying the book's concepts to your personal development, it's important to pause and congratulate yourself for embarking on thinking about where you may fit and where you may need more developmental focus. That is a testament to your use of emotional intelligence. Simply having the motivation to consider what you may need to be successful is noteworthy. And, by thinking about where you are and what you might need to better serve others, you are crossing multiple facets of the emotional intelligence competencies, bringing together your own self-awareness with your care for others and for your organization.

Stress, Multitasking, Conflict, and Communication

Growing our emotional intelligence can be a challenge in and of itself. It requires an extraordinary amount of vulnerability and inward thinking to do it well. Certainly in our personal lives there are opportunities for better self-awareness and self-management, perhaps even empathy. But they seem daunting. One way to make strong emotional intelligence feel more attainable, and understandable, is to couple it with real-world challenges that we face.

Thinking about developing our own skills is exciting! It gives us hope for the future and helps keep us stoke enthusiasm about the work that we do. Yet as much as I wish we could stay focused on the positives with regards to our own career development and the value of emotional intelligence, I would be remiss if I didn't address some of the stumbling blocks that we all face working in the talent development profession. We confront the real world all the time, and not every day is filled with a flawless execution of our curriculum design, support, or teaching skills. Sometimes, we experience situations where we find discomfort. This gets in the way of our ability to achieve our goals and serve our learners and clients.

- **Stress.** Stress creates an extraordinary amount of anxiety among us. Tight deadlines, difficult classroom interactions, and a shortage of resources will always put a damper on even the brightest day. Stress can affect us both psychologically and physically. And without addressing it, we run the risk of burnout or worse.

- **Multitasking.** Show me one talent development professional who doesn't multitask. It's easy to respond to a busy schedule by attempting to do too many things at one time. We juggle multiple social media platforms, laptops, and even in-person conversations at the same time. While we think this may be the answer to relieving our anxiety, it actually creates more tension in our lives and makes us less productive (see *stress*).

- **Conflict.** Conflict is much like stress. It is present in all aspects of our lives. However, it does not have to be a bad thing. In fact, conflict can yield innovation and creativity when handled well. But failing to identify and constructively address conflict can have unwanted physical and emotional impacts and create huge organizational problems.

- **Communication.** A world of stress, multitasking, and conflict does not offer the best environment for effective communication with those with whom we work. Indeed, communication is a common denominator of all our workplace challenges. How do we handle conversations with our learners? Do we put enough thought into the written communication that we produce? Do we pay any attention to our nonverbal cues?

Stress, multitasking, conflict, and communication are massively present in all the work we do as talent development professionals. They are a natural reaction to the challenges we face. We are simply human beings, imperfect and emotionally charged, and that is nothing to be ashamed of.

And this is where the magic of emotional intelligence comes to bear. Self-awareness gives us the tools to recognize when we're stressed, overtasked, in conflict, or communicating poorly. Self-regulation helps us gauge our reactions. Understanding our motivations keeps us moving forward and focused on goals. Empathy, especially in conflict and communication, offers that human touch, which lends a sense of caring to even the most difficult conversations. Finally, social skills are there for all to see, no matter the situation, offering a testament of our ability to connect, understand, and trust.

Wrap-Up

In the next few chapters, we're going to tackle each of these pesky challenges with a number of case studies, exercises, and tips. As you read, do your best to employ your most important emotional intelligence competency: your self-awareness! Look hard at yourself as you wander through the remainder of the book; think of the things that you do, and don't do. And please, this is not an indictment of you or your talent. We're just exploring. I see myself in every one of the following chapters, especially in the areas where I need improvement. Let's go through this together!

CHAPTER 5

Stress

Caitlin's Stress-Filled Day

It had been quite the day for Caitlin. Serving as a talent manager in a large nonprofit organization, she was working on so many projects that she lost track of time almost daily. Today had been particularly busy, with back-to-back Zoom meetings, a recruitment report due, and six résumés to review. She'd arrived at work ready to go. Then her hard drive had crashed. As the IT professionals descended on her office to help, her boss called her in to tell her she'd been selected to head up a new virtual talent recruitment initiative.

Our World of Stress

Our workforce is stressed out, and our failing grade on emotional intelligence is making things worse. We aren't self-aware enough to recognize the impact of stress, and our self-regulation skills can falter when we do feel the presence of stress in our lives. Our relationships and motivation suffer and our productivity drops. It's true that year after year, in survey after survey, employees consistently report that their jobs are stressful, and many consider their work to be one of the top stressors, if not the top stressor, in their lives. And most consider workplace stress to be worse now than ever before, and given the number of hours we're committing to work, perhaps that's true (Almeida et al. 2020). Does this sound like you?

When we think about an average workweek, we often think of the traditional eight-hour day. But this number is deceiving. Many find themselves working, or thinking about work, 16–18 hours each day, including weekends, holidays, and vacation days—in other words, every waking hour. Burnout and turnover have become the norm. The ever-increasing pressure to stay competitive has turned the 40-hour workweek into a thing of the past. We are attached to our phones, computers, and tablets from when we first wake up to well into the evening. How often do you check email outside your typical working hours? Do you clench up when you hear your device ping and worry that it's a work email, perhaps from a client asking for a last-minute change to a training program?

The 2020 *Stress in America* report, produced by the American Psychological Association (APA), paints a frightful picture of stress in our nation (APA 2020). To begin, only half of the workforce is comfortable discussing stress and other mental health issues. This is exceptionally troubling given the impact stress has on our mental well-being. When employees are fearful of bringing mental health issues to their supervisor, it affects their ability to feel supported and comfortable in the workplace. Sadly, the stigma often attached to these issues creates an inescapable trap for those suffering from stress. We have it. And when we don't talk about it, it gets worse!

🔆 Consider This

- How often do you talk honestly about stress with your co-workers? How about with your manager or with a coach?
- Do you ask your staff about their stress levels and their unique stressors? What about with the learners in your talent development programs?

In addition to a negative effect on well-being, the impact of stress in the workplace is unsurprisingly staggering, and the cost to companies with regards to turnover, lost productivity, and sick time is in the billions. Individuals suffering from stress-related disorders may be unable to complete tasks in a timely and focused manner. Work is often incomplete and not well planned. Their inability to focus creates challenges not only for their performance, but for the performance of those around them. Deadlines are missed, expectations go unfulfilled, and co-workers are left to make course corrections.

According to the American Institute of Stress, 83 percent of US workers endure some form of work-related stress, and on any given day up to 1 million people miss work because of stress. The cost? A whopping $300 billion yearly. To make matters worse, less than half of the workforce thinks their employers are concerned about work–life balance (American Institute of Stress 2020).

When organizations fail to deal with workplace stress in an effective way, they are destined for a lot of unwelcome outcomes. Because stress has a harmful effect on the body's immune system, workforces under extraordinary stress will have more sick days than those working in a more balanced environment. Turnover is likely to increase as well. Talented individuals want to work in organizations that are free flowing, trusting, welcoming, and fun to work at. They will quickly depart organizations that are marked by stressful interactions and tension. Likewise, recruiting to fill these positions becomes a challenge, creating even more problems for leadership.

A struggling economy and work insecurity are also creating stress. In 2020, the APA found that 70 percent of Americans have concerns about the economy, a 24 percent increase from the previous year. Those reporting nervousness and anxiety have more than doubled since 2018, and the COVID-19 pandemic, while not totally to blame for stress levels across the country, has had a significant impact as well, and not in a good way. Since the pandemic began, more than a third of Americans have begun showing signs of anxiety or depression.

The impact of these extraordinary levels of stress on the nation has been momentous. More people are having physical reactions to stress, along with showing clinical signs of anxiety and depression. Younger generations are struggling mightily as they attempt to build careers and pay off college debt. And for those who are besieged with mortgage or rent problems, the challenges are even more significant. Recent times have seen a massive increase in the numbers of Americans reaching out for help, whether it be to employers, nonprofits, or stress-related hotlines. We can't remove all the stressors from our lives, but through an effective use of emotional intelligence competencies and a few tips, we can mitigate stress tremendously. And in this chapter, I'll show how managing our response to stress is a critical aspect of developing your emotional intelligence skills.

What Is Stress?

Stress is common. It's the body's natural reaction to various types of events. As such, stress is a part of our daily lives, much like for Caitlin from the beginning of the chapter. From the moment we awake until the moment we can't sleep at night, stress is at play. Most stress has a tendency to resolve itself in the short term, typically in one or two days. For example, an instructional design report that is due on Friday will, thankfully, be finished by Friday! The stress building up to this event will then be resolved, and you'll get to enjoy your weekend. You might feel the same type of stress while planning an exciting upcoming vacation—you're making lists, checking passports, and ensuring everything is in order before leaving on your journey. Again, once the vacation is over, the stress dissipates. Stress is always there.

 Consider This
- When was the last time you experienced a stressful event?
- Were you aware of the stress as it happened or not until later?
- How did you feel in the moment?
- How would you gauge your self-regulation as you reacted?

Good Stress Versus Bad Stress

Stress can come in both welcome and unwelcome packages, which significantly affects our mental and physical well-being—sometimes in good ways, sometimes in not so good ways. Good stress would include the vacation example. Likewise, a new recruitment opportunity for an

Consider This

- When was the last time you felt good stress?
- How did you feel in the moment?
- How did you react?

organization could create stress for the recruiter. Excited about the possibilities that someone new could join the team, the recruiter stays focused and executes her role to perfection. This could include simple conversations with the candidate, a presentation, and answering questions. The recruiter prepares well, stays focused, and meets the challenge at hand.

From what in your life do you get good stress? Consider a time when you felt some stress that invigorated you—from an impending deadline, perhaps, or right before you had to facilitate a training session.

Bad stress is a different story altogether. Bad stress may include any number of personal or professional situations, such as being in a difficult family relationship, financial problems, or struggling with chronic illness. Working under a narcissistic boss would be another cause of bad stress, as is working in an environment where there's little appreciation for the work you do, or where internal organizational politics negatively affect your ability to complete job assignments. Unlike the benefits of good stress—increased focus, preparation—bad stress can negatively affect a number of our physiological and psychological functions.

What are your sources of bad stress? Is it a subject matter expert who always waits until the last moment to respond to your requests for training content, and thus leaves you with little time to revise? Is it a particular stakeholder who assumes you're available at all times to answer their training questions?

Acute Stress Versus Chronic Stress

The National Institute of Mental Health (NIMH) defines stress as falling into two prime categories: acute and chronic. As with good and bad stress, both acute and chronic stress have a significant influence on all of us.

Think of acute stress as pressure caused by a short-term project or temporary situation. This could be related to events that are about to occur in the future, or that recently occurred in the past. For a future event, a curriculum designer may have anxiety about the final draft of a proposal due next month. The idea of finalizing the details before presenting to a decision-making body would cause substantial stress. Similarly, the same designer may experience anxiety as a result of a presentation to the governing board that did not go well. The resultant stress of uncertainty about the quality of the product would likely stay with the designer for some time afterward.

Acute stressors are fluid. This type of pressure typically arrives on our life landscape as something new, or not resonant throughout our lives. These stressors come and go with the times, presenting themselves in a variety of ways in and out of the workplace. Luckily, many have fairly clear and easily applied solutions, ones that we have been trained to resolve as part of our professional growth. And this preparation does have a tendency to reduce the stress, a little.

Chronic stress has a darker side. Unlike acute stressors that pop in and out of life, chronic stressors are longer term in nature. Similar to bad stress, they may manifest as long-term economic insecurity, toxic work environments, or difficult and lasting family drama. If the curriculum designer described earlier is working in an environment where there is little trust, and unacceptable behavior from senior administrators is rampant, chronic stress will likely be in play. The tension inherent in simply reporting to work each day would cause extraordinary pressure.

The impact of chronic stress is more cumulative and, not surprisingly, more harmful. This is especially true when a person has suffered so long under the yoke of stress that they give up, and no longer work toward a solution.

Other Categorizations

Stress can manifest itself in many ways. Researchers note that stress can appear as a result of routine, sudden, or traumatic events. Routine stress would include the tasks we face each day: commuting, childcare, chores, financial responsibilities. Sudden stress appears as unexpected and unsettling events. These may include the loss of a job, or the death of a loved one. Finally, traumatic stress would involve life-changing events, such as a severe auto accident, an illness, an assault, war, or environmental disaster. All three affect us in real ways.

Frequency of Stress

In Caitlin's case, the causes of stress were work related and quite common. We've all had days like hers, ones when an unexpected computer failure, or an unanticipated new task from our boss, added to an already busy day. But stress makes its presence known in other parts of our lives as well. Whether it's a visit to the dentist, the purchase of a new car, or in-laws popping by the house unexpectedly, stress is part of being human. There is just no escaping it.

There are many ways to assess the presence of stress in our lives. One way is to ask ourselves tough questions and use our self-awareness to answer them. Take a look at the following list of questions. They are adapted from the Perceived Stress Scale, perhaps the most widely used tool for providing a snapshot of individual stress levels (Cohen, Kamarck, and Mermelstein 1983). Think about your answers and jot them down on the provided lines.

How often do you feel upset because something unexpected happened?

_____

_____

How often do you feel you've lost control of things in your life that are important to you?

_____

_____

How often are you nervous and stressed?

_____

_____

How confident are you about your ability to handle personal problems?

_____

_____

How often do you feel confident that things are going your way?

_____

_____

How often are you unable to cope with the things on your to-do list?

_____

_____

How often have you been able to control things that bug you?

_____

_____

How often do you feel on top of things?

_____

_____

How often have you been angry because things are outside your control?

_____

_____

How often have you thought that things were piling up so high that you could not overcome them?

_____

_____

Sometimes is a common answer to many of these questions. But if you find yourself using the phrases *a lot* or *often* or *every day*, you may be experiencing undue stress. We generally experience stress because we feel we are in danger, or out of control. We can also experience stress as a result of physical and emotional pain. In both cases, we often come to the conclusion that we don't have the resources to cope with the situation, which adds even more stress. This can happen in our personal lives too. Stress can manifest as a result of money worries, difficult relationships in and outside the home, or uncertainty about anything ranging from health to politics.

Events can also cause stress in our lives. Our learners fear examinations, reading loads, deadlines, balancing work and personal development, and leaving work undone while in the classroom. Those we recruit are concerned about moving to a new job, and leaving an old job, and the uncertainty of both. Make no mistake: Our colleagues deal with all the work and life challenges that we face. We are all in the stress mess together.

The Role of the Brain

As you would expect, the brain plays a role in stress. In particular, there is what scientists refer to as the discrepancy between an immediate return environment and a delayed return environment. In an immediate return environment, we see the results of our work and our tasks in real time. We make a decision to do something and we immediately, or in very short order, are able to observe its completion. A lesson plan is due; we prepare it; problem solved.

Immediate return environments go back to prehistoric times, when immediate gratification and success were necessary for survival, and they continue to blend well with our human tendency for constancy and predictability. We like to know that what we have done has made a difference, and we like to see that difference. When we do so, there is an almost instantaneous impact on life. So, we do well when we remain focused on the present or the very near future.

But things have changed a lot since the days of our hunter-gatherer descendants. We have much more information surrounding us to inform our decisions. We also have cultural and societal expectations of immediate and demonstrable success. Unfortunately, these do not always blend with the complexity of the workplace, the general demands of life, and a serious scarcity of time to see things to their natural conclusion. Projects take time to develop and implement. We don't always get to see our results immediately.

Welcome to the delayed return environment. We are now in a world where the decisions we make today may have an impact so far down the line, and across so many spheres, it is virtually impossible to relish in their success. The immediate results are simply not present. They are long term. And they depend on other factors, many of which may be out of our control. This is where we can lean on the motivation dimension of emotional intelligence. Recognizing our own motivations and finding comfort in what drives us will help us through the delayed return that we experience in most of our decision making today.

Personality Traits

Personality traits may contribute to stress as well; research suggests that people with certain traits are more likely to have anxiety (Lecic-Tosevski and Vukovic 2011).

Perfectionism

Think of the perfectionist in your life—they struggle with anxiety because by their nature they are looking for order in a world of disorder. This endless search fuels anxiety because a perfectionist attempts to do the perfect work, and when they fail as we all often do, they become tense. This tension fuels the possibility of more mistakes, which makes the perfectionist even more anxiety-ridden. This cycle is difficult to escape.

Analysis Paralysis

A similar outcome occurs with those who engage in analysis paralysis. We all have a colleague who overthinks everything. They obsess over every detail for every decision, often returning back to an original thinking pattern, and back again, and again, yielding frustration in those around them and unnecessary delays in getting the work done. This causes anxiety not only in the overthinker, but also in colleagues who depend on their work to achieve organizational objectives.

Worry

Some of us are just worriers by nature, and this can be a significant cause of stress in our lives. While it is perfectly normal to worry on occasion, some are plagued by an incessant and debilitating tendency to worry. These individuals may struggle with what physicians term *generalized anxiety disorder*. People with this disorder, many of whom develop it during their teenage years, worry all the time about everything. As children, we might fret over how well we perform in school, social interactions, or larger global catastrophes. During adulthood, the worrying falls into categories we might expect: finances, health, jobs. The worrying may also extend to more mundane things, like simply being late to a meeting.

Caring

It does seem strange, but caring can actually contribute to stress in our lives. Well, caring too much! People who are overly empathetic have a tendency to focus on the people around them to the detriment of their own well-being. They care so much about making other people comfortable and looking after their needs, that they tend to avoid their own. They hold themselves accountable for the happiness and emotional health of others, and experience extreme anxiety when they fail.

Resistance to Change

This is a very difficult personality trait for individuals working in the talent development world. The talent development professional landscape is a changing one and creates demands on professionals. There are resource barriers, challenges with finding the right talent, and debate about the most effective educational andragogy. Further, the field is always changing, and while resistance to change creates substantial barriers for organizational success, it also generates anxiety in individuals who tend to avoid change. People suffering from this fear are uncomfortable and frightened when faced with something new. They tend to overthink and focus on the potential negative outcomes of change, generating high levels of anxiety and tension.

Reactions and Impact

We all react differently to stress. Sometimes what causes stress for one individual will have no impact on another. The determinants involved in what causes a reaction to stress can include something as easily identifiable as a personality trait. People who possess one of the previously described personality traits, such as overthinking, would more likely be stressed out by the introduction of a new business process in the workplace. Likewise, someone with a more laid-back approach to life might see this new introduction as just another day at the office.

Of course, history also plays a role in how we react to stressful situations. People growing up in environments where stress was handled in a calm and rational approach are often better suited to deal with tension as they mature. Individuals who experience difficulties handling stress at a young age will struggle with stress if they do not develop the coping mechanisms to do so. One thing is certain, our individual reactions to stress are as unique as we are.

When we do react to stress, it may manifest in a physical or mental form. Our physical reaction is a symphony of neurochemistry, and it happens in an instant. We begin by producing cortisol, epinephrine, and norepinephrine. As a result, our blood pressure and pulse increase quickly. We become more alert and focused. Also, our muscles are inclined to tighten, as if to prepare for protection. Skin tends to flush and sweat glands are activated. Interestingly, other systems in the body begin to shut down as we become more stressed. Our digestive system stops sending signals of hunger and slows the gastric breakdown of foods in our stomach. Likewise, our immune system activity begins to decrease. All of this allows for a laser focus on the momentary stressor in our lives. What are some of the ways you've noticed that you physically express stress?

 Consider This
- Think about how you react when you are under stress. Write it down.
- Ask three friends to describe how they see you react when you're under stress. Write their responses down.
- Compare the lists. Are there any differences?

From a mental perspective, our emotional reactions are just as significant. Stress can create concentration challenges, even for the most menial task. Because of our focus on the stressor at hand, we can become irritable and forgetful, slowly disconnecting from those around us as we struggle to deal with the anxiety. Those under significant stress may feel anger, fatigue, or hopelessness. This may result in a variety of behaviors including emotional outbursts, crying, social withdrawal, or substance abuse. In short, the emotional toll of stress is monumental.

Managing Your Stress

The hard facts regarding the impact stress has on individuals and organizations serve as a wake-up call for the importance of the psychological health of the workforce now and in the future. Creating environments of kindness and trust is a strong foundation for addressing these challenges. Likewise, well-funded employee assistance programs and wellness resources, positioned to meet a workforce's unique needs, can go a long way in providing the support that talent development professionals need.

On a personal level, consider the following practices to reduce stress levels:

- **Be real.** It's not real to have unreal expectations about what we can accomplish. Use self-awareness as your main tool to recognize and own your limits and allow plenty of time to write that lesson plan, or prep for that meeting. Unexpected interruptions always occur, so be generous with yourself.

- **Organize yourself.** Write it down. Keep a list, in priority order, of the things you need to get done and mark them off as you do. (Trust me, it will make you feel good as you line through that newly completed task!) Simply getting these on paper is relief in itself. And learn to say no, then delegate anything you can.

- **Relax.** Whether it's reading, meditating, gardening, going to the gym, whatever floats your boat. Ask yourself what you would do on a Saturday morning if you had nothing to do—no deadlines, nobody bugging you—and then do it. It's probably what relaxes you the most! Schedule time on your calendar to do more of it each day or week.

- **Think positively and laugh a little.** The emotional intelligence construct of motivation is a natural source of positivity. Our outlook matters. When we frame the world in a positive light, we feel less stress and see more possibilities for happiness. And don't forget the amazing power of humor. A little chuckle here and there lowers stress levels and connects us with others. What are the sources of positivity or laughter in your life? Is it a sibling, colleague, or barista at your favorite coffee shop? An app, a television show, or a pop culture blog? Can you tap into them more often?

- **Seek help.** We're never alone, even if we feel like it in the most stressful times. Lean on your support network, friends, and family.

And don't hesitate to reach out to a counselor or psychotherapist if you feel the need. Just don't ignore it. If you feel it, it's real.

Practice Point—Face It Head On!

As much as we would like it to be different, stress is always going to be around. Whether it is preparation for that complex lecture or hanging out with in-laws who don't like you, by directly addressing the cause of stress and taking active steps to resolve it, we can be prepared for anything that life tosses our way.

Imagine for a moment that you've been on an amazing vacation in the islands for the last 10 days. Sailing, sunning, swimming, you name it. (Or if snowcapped mountains are more your jam, chilling in the lodge after a day of skiing. Pick your spot and activity.) You have had a terrific time. No stress. You finally feel more relaxed than you've ever felt in as long as you can remember. The biggest stressor you had your entire vacation was what to do for dinner. How nice!

But you do have to get back to work because you have a significant amount on your plate—facilitating, coaching, designing, leading. And while it is something that you enjoy doing, you are finding your thoughts slowly creeping back to the office. You still have almost two full days left, but you've now opened the floodgates by allowing work to invade your bliss. You are an extremely self-aware individual, so you know this is happening. You can feel it physically, and it's ruining your remaining time in paradise. You need to do something.

A few key steps:

- You've already accomplished one of the most significant tasks in front of you. You have used your self-awareness, identified the things that trigger your stress, and faced them directly. Just knowing what it is on your mind and contributing to your anxiety is a strong first step toward dealing with it effectively. Congratulate yourself. The triggers that we avoid thinking about or don't recognize are the ones that cause the most problems where stress is concerned. Now that we're here, we are poised to self-regulate our response.

- Make a list of exactly what you are stressed about. In this case, you have a very full teaching schedule. This has already been established. But what is it precisely about the upcoming classes that is making you avoid that extra piña colada? Is it the technical support in the classroom? Is it the availability of materials? Is it the composition of the learners in the room? Jot these down and give your brain a chance to build a little space. The brain will work on these problems even when you are not thinking about them. Writing them down gives you a sense of accomplishment and motivation and keeps you from worrying about what you may be forgetting.

- Remember where you are and use the amazing surroundings and memories to refocus your brain in a positive direction. You've already written down what you were concerned about, so there's no reason to think about it any longer. Save that for the flight home. By focusing on the experiences that you were having, it makes it easier to refocus your neurological resources toward a more positive mindset. Try something new and adventurous in the last couple of days to take your mind off your return to work. Better yet, plan your next vacation before you leave your current one. See how that works? Stress can't win!

Wrap-Up

Stress is no joke. It can affect us in so many ways, both personally and professionally. Untended, stress can impair our ability to not only be self-aware, but also recognize others' needs and communicate effectively with them. Our ability to be an effective talent development professional suffers as well. Stress can have a devastating impact on our effectiveness in instructional design and delivery. Our productivity decreases, and our organizations suffer.

As a reminder, note the role that emotional intelligence plays in the world of stress:

- Self-awareness allows us to recognize that we are under stress, along with being aware of its influence on our bodies, thinking, and relationships.
- When practiced well, self-regulation provides the opportunity to use tools to deal with stress and modify our attitudes and behaviors.
- You can tap into your intrinsic motivation as a way to deal with stress. However, motivation can also be negatively affected by stress.
- As with motivation, our ability to be empathetic can be damaged by excessive stress levels.
- Often the most visible outward sign of too much stress is when we're unable to communicate with our colleagues, and when our social skills start to suffer.

While we can't eliminate stress in our lives, we can manage it. By recognizing the origin of stress and using some of the tips outlined in this chapter, we are in a much better position to manage something that is part of every hour of our daily lives. Organizing ourselves, setting schedules, keeping to-do lists, and taking a little time to relax are guaranteed to combat stress. But as we work to deal with stress in our lives, just beware of a common and often ineffective strategy—multitasking. It may feel like it's working, but not so much. Read on!

CHAPTER 6
Multitasking

Quinn Is Juggling Too Many Things!

As the primary learning and development lead, Quinn often found herself busier than she could have imagined. In the middle of any given day, you could find her at her dual-screen desk computer, learner data on one screen and a new curriculum design on the other, while she texted a co-worker. Toss in the occasional call from her office phone, and you could argue that Quinn was definitely, shall we say, engaged! But it wasn't just at work. She always seemed to have lots going on. Even when her nephew, Fox, would FaceTime his favorite aunt and ask her to read him a story, which she loved doing, she would do so while checking her email and folding laundry. Whether she was reading a novel while on the exercise bike or navigating multiple website browser tabs on her tablet while eating dinner, Quinn was a multitasker. She was also exhausted.

Our Love of Multitasking

Let's be honest about something. You're multitasking while reading this chapter. Aren't you? That's what makes writing about multitasking so easy. We all do it; sometimes we realize, and sometimes we don't. In fact, I'm doing it now! I like to think I excel at listening to music from Spotify playing quietly in the background, watching a Netflix series blaring away, chatting hands-free on my cell phone, and typing a chapter on multitasking all at once. How apropos.

With that out of the way, I want you to stop everything you're doing at this very moment and take heed of what's around you. My guess is, if you're like me, you at the very least have a book in your hand, your laptop open, and your phone nearby. If you're at home, you may also have a television on or be listening to music. There is the ever-present sound of new text messages arriving, and you may have family or friends near you. In the workplace, the presence of multitasking does not look that different. We pay attention to laptops (with multiple browsers open) and cell phones while in meetings, all the time, at the very same time. We take work phone calls while driving. We attend Zoom sessions while writing a report on the other screen. We sneak a peek at our email during a staff meeting. I'm guilty, too. Multitasking seems like the only approach we really have to accomplish all we must accomplish in our busy lives.

And like Quinn, we're exhausted.

Why We Multitask

We multitask for many reasons. It is no secret that deadlines seem to be shorter than ever before. There is a greater demand for productivity in the workplace. Curriculums need to be written, talent needs to be recruited, and budgets need to be developed. And it was all due yesterday. And in terms of resources, well, what are those again? They seem to be as scarce as ever. All of this demands that we find creative ways to manage ever-growing workloads while keeping ourselves as emotionally stable as possible.

We also multitask because of a lack of self-awareness and self-regulation. Yes, emotional intelligence plays a role here. As you will recall, self-awareness allows us to sense emotions and anxiety before we react to them. When we feel overwhelmed, we often attempt to multitask to accomplish more. When we have those inner signals of anxiety because of an unanticipated workload, we then lean on our self-regulation skills to tackle the task at hand. When we lack these two critical emotional intelligence competencies, we tend to multitask.

Lots of us multitask. OK, all of us multitask. Studies note that 99 percent of adults use two forms of media concurrently at some point during the week (Hammond 2016). We check our phones constantly, up to six times an hour, according to some estimates. We also get distracted easily. And while precise numbers on how many of us multitask are difficult to pin down, we do know that only 2 percent of the population can do it well (Sundem 2012). Most of us don't, and in the end, it creates problems.

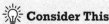
Consider This
- Have you ever felt overwhelmed?
- When was the last time you multitasked?
- How do you feel during and after you've multitasked?
- Have you ever had a negative interaction with a colleague because you felt overwhelmed?
- Do you see yourself as an effective multitasker?

Given the scientific evidence, it is justly amazing that we still find such comfort in multitasking. In fact, we rarely admit that we are not multitasking. We own it. We're proud of it. Look how much I can do at one time! Focusing, truly focusing, on one task at a time is quite rare in today's world. And while we might find an artificial joy in being able to juggle many things at once, we often fail to recognize the cost of such activity, both personally and professionally. Hence the need to examine the concept of multitasking, or perhaps the myth of multitasking, in a little more detail. Does it truly work? Is it different for different people? Is it having an impact that we don't recognize?

Don't answer all those questions at once. That would be multitasking!

Multitasking Is a Misnomer

Multitasking is an equal opportunity offender. Quinn did it. You do it. We all do it. Research suggests that there are no gender differences. There are no significant generational differences either (Beaton 2017). Even that sharp Gen Z-er working on e-learning design in the cubicle next to you suffers from the consequences of attempting to multitask.

I can hear you now: "But I'm different. I can juggle a lot of things at once." Well, let's check it out. A commonly used, very simple test easily shows what happens when we multitask.

Begin by drawing two horizontal lines on a piece of paper. Get a friend to time you as you do the following (no cheating):

1. Start the clock.
2. On the first line, write: *I am a great multitasker*.
3. On the second line, write out the numbers 1–20 sequentially:
   1 2 3 4 5 6 7 8 9 10 11 12 13 14 15 16 17 18 19 20.
4. Stop the clock.

Now check your time. The average adult is able to accomplish this task in approximately 20 seconds.

Let's try this again, but this time we'll multitask. On a new piece of paper, draw two more horizontal lines and get your friend to time you again.

1. Start the clock.
2. On the first line, write the first letter of *I am a great multitasker*.
3. On the second line, write the first number of the sequence of 1–20.
4. Repeat with the second letter of *I am a great multitasker* on the first line (a), and the second number in the sequence on the second line (2).
5. Continue switching back and forth until the sentence and the number sequence are complete.

How much time did that take you? Double the amount of time? Triple? This is what happens when we think we are multitasking. You more than likely made a few mistakes, had a couple of pauses, and had to think about where you were in your effort.

There's no argument that multitasking appears good on the surface—we believe we're accomplishing more. One of the reasons for that is we are touching different tasks throughout our multitasking experience. We spend a little time on one thing, and then we move to another, then another. This resonates with us because we, at least in our minds, are covering a lot of ground. But we're not. Let's take a look at what's really happening when we think we're multitasking; we'll follow along with Nikki, a talent development professional.

Multitasking

It was accreditation time again, and Nikki had a critical deadline for prepping documents that would be included in the final submission. She spent the entire day at her desk, assessing learning objectives and mapping them accordingly. Meanwhile she kept an eye on her phone for incoming email. One never knew what might pop up.

Here's a simple but powerful example of multitasking. We can easily define multitasking as endeavoring to do two or more things simultaneously. In this example, Nikki was balancing the preparation of accreditation documents with her email inbox. We all do it, trying to squeeze the most out of our workdays. It feels good, like we are accomplishing more than we truly are. So we keep on doing it.

Even with deadlines, when focusing on one task at a time is paramount for quality productivity, we find it hard not to attempt to multitask. Research suggests that workers spend just over 40 percent of their day multitasking with email and messaging. What's worse? Almost 19 percent can't last more than 20 minutes before resorting to some form of electronic communication medium (MacKay 2018).

Context Switching

Nikki is at it again. This time she is preparing a PowerPoint presentation for her boss, the department head of the training division. The problem is, she's scheduled to teach a class the next day and is woefully behind on her facilitation notes. She decides she'll work on the boss's presentation for 45 minutes, then switch over to her notes and try to make some headway there. Each time she attempts the switch, it always takes her a minute to assess where she left off and what needs to still be done. This cycle goes on most of the day.

Context switching is aptly named. It occurs when we shift back and forth between tasks. This is precisely what happened in the "I am a great multitasker" exercise from earlier. We think we're doing two things at once, but all we're really doing is switching from task to task to task. Each time we do, it takes a moment to regain our sense of where we are on that task. That's lost time, and it takes a toll on our ability to concentrate.

The impact of context switching is backed up by research that suggests the more tasks we assume, the less productive we become. If we have the discipline to concentrate on one task at a time, we harness up to 100 percent of our productive time. If we try to tackle two tasks, we capture only 40 percent of our productivity for each task, and juggling three tasks at a time reduces our productive time for each task to 20 percent (MacKay 2019).

Attention Residue

Nikki finally finished her facilitation notes and the PowerPoint presentation for her boss. At work the next day, she was ready to go for her class while her boss presented to a group of potential investors down the hall. But something wasn't right. Nikki's class notes were incomplete. She had left out several critical learning objectives that needed to be covered in class that day. Meanwhile, her boss started texting her in the afternoon demanding to know why the PowerPoint slides were missing crucial financial information that she needed to make her case to organizational stakeholders.

Attention residue occurs when we attempt to perform a number of tasks in sequence, typically quickly. Researcher Sophie Leroy (2009) coined this term in her research to describe how we often need to manage multiple projects or tasks at the same time. We react by context switching, but there's a catch. It turns out there's a significant neurological challenge to tackling multiple projects in sequence, especially when we fail to fully complete a task before moving to another. When we fail to totally finish a job, it is difficult for us to turn our complete attention to the new task. The residual thought patterns from the previous task remain embedded in our brains, keeping us from devoting our full thought to the next one.

The Impact of Multitasking

Multitasking must feel productive if so many of us participate in it. But is it? What impact does multitasking actually have on our work?

Poor Time Management

Many of us struggle mightily with our time management skills. That said, most of us give ourselves tremendous credit for being excellent time managers. There's no need to feel bad; time management is difficult. At best, we have a fundamental misunderstanding of what time it is anyway. We often think of time as something we can control. In truth, we can't. Time continues to move with or without us. Whether we are doing something or not, the clock continues to tick. Deadlines approach. History happens.

We think we manage time well because of our comfort with multitasking. The fact is that multitasking does not help with our time management; it makes it worse. Even though we think we may be more productive, we are not. We spend more time jumping back and forth between tasks than actually completing them. This results in rework and incomplete efforts, which mean, you guessed it, more rework.

Depending on multitasking to solve our time management problems is a recipe for disaster. It can lead to any number of significant impacts on our health and well-being, such as anxiety and lack of sleep. When we have many unfinished tasks, we tend to lie awake or wake up in the middle of the night thinking of those tasks. Even our diet can be affected as we attempt to make the best use of our limited time by eating unhealthy meals. We grab a quick bite on the way out the door to our next meeting without allowing time for even the most modest break.

Difficulty Concentrating

Look back at our discussion on attention residue, and it follows that something must be neurologically awry where multitasking is concerned. Task switching, interruptions, and external noise all affect the way the brain thinks and our ability to focus on one task at a time. Every time we stop and start again, it draws on our neurological resources. This affects what researchers refer to as *flow*, a psychological term that denotes being in a state of high mental performance—that is, being in the zone. In flow, we are completely focused on the task that we are attempting to accomplish. In the training world, think about when you're preparing a lesson plan and you're on a roll, connecting ideas and concepts smoothly and efficiently. This results in more productive time than when you are context switching or experiencing other interruptions.

Memory may be affected as well. A 2018 study assessed the influence various media technologies may have on human cognition. In other words, was there was a relationship between media multitasking and memory? The answer was yes (Uncapher and Wagner 2018). The findings show that heavier media multitaskers struggled in several critical domains. Most important, their short-term working memory was affected as they switched from task to task. This ultimately leads to increased anxiety as we struggle to stay focused. Our brains continue this cycle of one step forward and two steps back. And because our brains are expending so much neurological capital in jumping back and forth, both our innovation and creativity suffer.

Loss of Productivity

Think for a moment about the dynamics that occur when we sit down to tackle a particular task at work. We have the activity itself, the amount of time necessary to complete the activity, and our mental and physical state when undertaking the task. But we also have the environment to consider. Is it a large office with lots of background noise? Are you in a cubicle? A private space? We must also take into account the likelihood of interruption, and the type of interruption (phone call, text message, visitor). The importance of the interruption matters as well. Is it a critical matter that demands our attention, or a trivial matter that could have waited? Either produces attention residue with which we must deal, and once again, we waste resources attempting to get back on task.

All of these factors combine to spell downtime. Distracting background noise causes us to lose focus. Interruptions occur, delaying our work even further and causing us to pause for a few minutes to figure out where we were before the delay. Our own attention spans come into play as well. We can typically stay focused on a task for only 10 minutes or so before moving to another task (Wilson and Korn 2007). When we do, productivity suffers to the tune of millions of dollars a year (Steinhorst 2020).

On the Positive Side

We'll probably never stop multitasking. Our fast-paced and quickly changing environments place all of us in a position that, at the very least, makes us feel the need to multitask. And it does give us a sense of satisfaction, even if the data suggests that our productivity is less than optimal. But is there room for multitasking, ever? The answer is yes.

 Consider This
- What are three activities you regularly do where you feel safe multitasking?
- Do any of them involve a moving vehicle? (Please say no!)
- Do they involve other people?

Perhaps you listed things such as folding laundry, drying dishes, filing, or paying bills. Any of these could be categorized aptly as mundane, routine, even boring. They require little attention (although perhaps a tad more focus is needed when paying bills). Many times, they come in combinations of two. I often fold laundry while watching television, or listen to music while gardening. Either way, these are tasks that seldom use lots of brainpower. In these cases, multitasking can work.

There are also a few, a precious few, who are what scientists call super-taskers. David Strayer and Jason Watson (2010) of the University of Utah coined this term when they were investigating whether cell phone use in a car is more dangerous than talking to a passenger who's in the car with you. (Turns out, cell phone use is more dangerous, so put the phone down!) What they discovered was the few, the proud, the 2 percent of the population who are able to divide their concentration safely and effectively. Let's just say I'm not one of them, and you're probably not either.

How to Avoid Multitasking

Changing your habits and putting a stop to multitasking is not going to be easy. I won't sugarcoat it: Even after writing this chapter, I still find myself reaching down and checking my phone while working on something else. You've likely done so a few times while reading this chapter. Still, there are several ways we can avoid multitasking and become more productive along the way:

- **Use self-awareness and self-regulation.** One of the powers of emotional intelligence is that it allows us to recognize our behaviors and adjust them before we actually take action. In the case of multitasking, self-awareness gives us the tools to sense that we are becoming overwhelmed, and self-regulation allows us to adjust our habits so that we focus on one thing at a time.
- **Build your fortress to stay motivated.** Many of the challenges we face regarding multitasking are related to our environment, which can contribute just as much to our slippage into multitasking as our own thought patterns. If you can't stand to be away from your phone, turn the volume off or put it in airplane mode and turn it upside down. Close your door. Let everyone know that you need one hour of uninterrupted time to focus on the task at hand.
- **Use a timer to help self-regulate.** If you must switch between tasks, use a timer to allow you to maintain focus on one before moving to another. When working on a particular project, try to

stay focused on that project for at least 40 minutes before moving to the next task. This will lessen the impact of attention residue.

- **Give yourself a break.** The influence of attention residue is lowered when we all take breaks in between our tasks. Try different approaches! Some can work for 25 minutes or more, take a break, and feel completely relieved. Others prefer, once they have reached the state of flow, to work longer and then take a longer break. There is no perfect answer, but doing this well has a positive impact on our motivation. Simply practice different methods and stick with the one that works.

- **Let your email wait.** One of the most significant causes of multitasking is our undisciplined need to constantly check our email. Use a software tracker on your email to tell you how much time you spend in your inbox each day. There may be room for adjustment in the number of times you check your messages, and the amount of time you spend on them. Make sure that you're not included in email strings that don't require your attention. Unnecessary emails distract us and take time to process. You may consider limiting your email time and working in "bursts" to answer the ones you need to.

- **Do one thing at a time.** As counterintuitive as it seems, we know that focusing on one project (or one person) at a time allows you to be more productive and socially connected. It also stimulates ingenuity and originality because you are able to think clearly about the task in front of you. Do your best to "single task," stay disciplined, and allow yourself to get into a state of flow. Turn to the next task only when the current task is completed.

Practice Point—Schedule Your Day!

With all of the work that a typical talent development professional needs to accomplish, it's no wonder that we aren't self-aware. We get lost and overwhelmed, and respond by attempting to multitask our way out of very busy days. We try to write lesson plans while covering our email and answering phone calls. We spend time looking for the latest literature for our classrooms while reviewing evaluation data. The list goes on.

Working from a schedule can be an effective technique in dealing with our increasing workload. By using calendars and to-do lists, we relieve our brain of thinking of all the things that we must accomplish. In essence, we create space in our mind to stay organized and use our brainpower for more innovative purposes instead of fighting the battle with attention residue and trying to keep track of all that is in front of us. It's self-regulation at its finest.

I found that, the old-fashioned day-timer planner approach worked well for me. If I looked at a month-at-a-glance page, I could see what was waiting for me over the next several weeks. This was a huge motivational tool because I believed I had command of what was about to happen. I could prepare in advance and be ready for anything that came my way. I have since entered the digital world and now use my phone fairly effectively as my calendar. However, I still write a to-do list that I keep within close range. By writing down what I need to accomplish, I can easily stop thinking about what I need to accomplish. All I need to do is look at the list!

A few key steps:

- Begin with self-awareness and recognize that multitasking is addicting. At the beginning of each week, devote 15 minutes to look into your schedule for the next five workdays and take note of what you have coming your way. Pay particular attention to calendar entries that require extra preparation.
- Ensure that your schedule includes both focused time for work on particular projects, and open time that will allow you to have some flexibility. This will keep you motivated throughout the day.
- Keep a to-do list that is prioritized based on your upcoming events. No need to rewrite this list every day. Simply cross out the items as they are completed. It feels really good!

- Each morning, look at your calendar for the day and cross-reference it with your to-do list. Some of the items may be related to that day's events; others may be in preparation for future events. For example, you might make note of the need to prepare for delivering training three days down the line. Regardless, comparing your upcoming day with your list of things to do will tell you exactly what you need to accomplish to be prepared.

- At the end of each day, glance at your calendar so you will know if you are prepared for the following day. Confirming that you are ready to go for the next round of work allows you to feel good about your day, enjoy your downtime, and relax a little each evening. Pair it perfectly, and responsibly, with some Chilean wine or an alternate beverage of choice!

Wrap-Up

Multitasking is here to stay. As much as we would all like to claim that we are going to tame this beast, we are unlikely to be 100 percent successful. If you are one of the 2 percent of the population that is a supertasker, congratulations! For the rest of us, our workload, our propensity for context switching, and our surroundings create a welcome environment for multitasking. It is no wonder that we so eagerly participate.

Still, using the tips in this chapter, we can make the most of our productive time and use those precious hours to create talent development materials that inspire and mold professionals across multiple industries. With just a few minor adjustments in our focus, our calendars, and our to-do lists, we can have more productive time than we ever imagined. We will also be happier, more balanced, and more effective in our work.

As a reminder, note the role that emotional intelligence plays in the world of multitasking:

- Self-awareness allows us to recognize that we all have the tendency to try to do too much at once, resulting in multitasking.

- When practiced well, self-regulation provides the opportunity to use tools to deal with multitasking and modify our habits and behaviors.
- By not multitasking, we are able to finish tasks correctly the first time, efficiently and completely. This sense of satisfaction fuels our motivation to complete the next task.
- Our ability to be empathetic can be damaged by excessive multitasking when we grow frustrated by our inability to complete our work.
- Our social skills suffer significantly when we multitask—such as when we fail to pay direct attention to those with whom we are speaking.

Lastly, avoiding multitasking allows us to develop an especially important skill—the ability to focus. It not only benefits us in the work we do, but also enhances our ability to communicate with others. Not allowing our mind to stray, and not checking our phones, can send a strong message to those with whom we communicate. Want to know more? Read on!

CHAPTER 7

Communication

Riley and Cale's Conversation

As a seasoned instructional systems designer with more than 30 years of experience, Riley was quite talented at creating training programs that worked well across a wide variety of subjects. Her classroom products were innovative and successful so long as facilitators paid close attention to the nuances of her unusual but creative approaches. When evaluations came back indicating that Cale, one of her newest facilitators, was struggling, it became clear that she needed to have a conversation with him. Unfortunately, communication between the two of them did not flow. Riley attempted to make her points clear but came off as bossy and insensitive. Cale, meanwhile, shy by nature, withdrew from the conversation and refused to make eye contact. When he did, he sent a very strong message that he did not appreciate Riley's intrusion on his facilitation style.

Communicating About Communication

It is so obvious, isn't it? Communication is a challenge. In fact, songwriters and performers have been writing and playing music about a lack of communication in relationships for as long as any of us has been alive. Just listen to any popular song. There's always an underlying theme of communication or lack thereof. Ego gets in the way of our simple need to share with each other. Relationships start, relationships get damaged, and relationships get rebuilt—all on the shoulders of communication.

It makes sense that the constructs of emotional intelligence would play a huge role in the way we communicate with one another. Self-awareness and regulation give us an indication of how well we recognize and deal with communication issues in ourselves and others. We are more motivated when we work in environments where communication is plentiful. There's more trust and empathy. And our social interactions are positive and supporting.

Communication pervades all that we do. No matter what the environment, we always have to communicate in some way with someone. We order products online by communicating with a customer service representative. We go to a coffee shop and communicate with the person at the counter. We communicate with other drivers while en route from point A to point B. We communicate when we send an email or post an Instagram photo. Everywhere, anywhere, all the time, we communicate.

The workplace is an especially thought-provoking environment for this element. Communication is of course necessary for building relationships and trust across teams. It is also important for imparting a vision or direction when we are in supervisory roles. It matters when we are sharing ideas and brainstorming with colleagues. Communication can occur in large groups during presentations, in small team meetings, or in one-on-one sessions. It can be through written, verbal, or nonverbal means.

When communication is done well, emotional intelligence is at play. Individuals use their self-awareness to monitor their emotional reactions to messages and their self-regulation to gauge their responses. We are able to be empathetic and understanding in multiple social contexts. Not only do we feel more trust and connection with one another, but we have a sense of belonging and satisfaction in the work we do. Good communication bonds us together. Our organizations become fluid and responsive, benefiting from a culture of openness.

When problems with communication exist, the opposite occurs. People put up boundaries and relationships dwindle. Trust dissolves and communication stops. Organizations become hollow entities with no soul and an organizational culture emerges that's ripe for complaints, absenteeism, and turnover. Productivity suffers and so do people.

> ### ✴ Consider This
> • Have you ever worked in an environment where communication was lacking?
> • How did it make you feel?
> • Was there an absence of empathy or motivation in the environment?
> • Did you ever want to avoid going to work because of it?

To be fair, communication is not easy, in part because of the many ways that we communicate and the many steps to do so. We have the message, the sender, the environment, and the receiver. There is intention, decoding, understanding, and acknowledging. The pathway matters as well. Some of us are better at writing, some of us are better at face-to-face discussions, some of us are better at presenting in groups, and some of us would rather die than stand up in front of a room full of people. Indeed, the number of venues for communicating a message is staggering, and if we can master one or two of them, we're probably in pretty good shape.

Answer the following questions by circling *yes, no,* or *sometimes,* and let's see where you stand in terms of your communication skills:

Before communicating, I consider any aspects of my message that may be misunderstood and think about how I will deal with that.	*yes*	*no*	*sometimes*
I customize the delivery method of my message based on my audience.	*yes*	*no*	*sometimes*
I am a good listener.	*yes*	*no*	*sometimes*
I welcome feedback.	*yes*	*no*	*sometimes*
I follow up to make sure my message was clear and understood.	*yes*	*no*	*sometimes*

Most of us, if answering honestly, will say *sometimes* to these questions. That does not mean we are bad human beings. It simply tells us that there is room for improvement in how we communicate with one another.

How We Communicate

Communication comes in three forms—verbal, nonverbal, and written—and the tenets of emotional intelligence influence all of them. When put that way, it may be comforting to know that you have to deal with only three different types of communication, but the fact is that even with only three, the gradations are staggering. Each has its own unique challenges and requires a specific set of skills to do well.

Verbal Communication

Verbal communication is fraught with significant challenges for both the communicator and the receiver. The words that we use and the way that we put them together to communicate our message can endear or offend our intended listener. Using inclusive and culturally sensitive language will help bridge the communication gap, especially when we are attempting to be empathetic. However, using language that is offensive (profane or gender-bound) is certain to create problems. For example, exhibiting a lack of self-awareness by referring to a room full of people as *guys* ("Hey guys, thanks for attending my presentation today") may get us off on the wrong foot. Even something as simple as using unfamiliar acronyms can be seen as a microaggression and damage our ability to communicate our message.

Tone plays a major role in verbal communication as well, especially in the way that we choose to emphasize particular words. From a social skills perspective, this can be evident to anyone listening in. For example, consider the following exchange (emphasis in italics):

Chelsea did not tell Drisana that our training session was canceled. *(Meaning: Someone else did.)*

Chelsea did not tell *Drisana* that our training session was canceled.
(Meaning: Maybe Chelsea told someone else.)

Chelsea did not tell Drisana that *our training session* was canceled.
(Meaning: But something else may have been.)

Chelsea did not tell Drisana that our training session was *canceled*.
(Meaning: Perhaps it was simply delayed.)

Chelsea did not *tell* Drisana that our training session was canceled.
(Meaning: Chelsea was only implying it may be canceled.)

By focusing on the emphasis of specific words, we can see that the meaning is significantly altered. Add to this dynamic a tone of voice that may be interpreted as flustered or angry, and we can see how the role of emotional intelligence influences the ultimate path of this conversation. If we're being an empathetic listener and cautious with our emotions, all we need to do is ask a clarifying question to understand what the statement truly means.

And verbal communication is not limited to face-to-face any longer. The verbal communication dynamics of today also include a number of media platforms in and out of the classroom, such as Zoom or FaceTime.

Nonverbal Communication

Far more complex than the verbal method, nonverbal communication plays a major part in how we message one another. Research over the last 50 years has suggested that anywhere from 70 to 93 percent of our communication comes from nonverbal means (Smith 2020). The impact of this is that despite what we say, or the tone we use, the way we say it nonverbally matters. Avoiding eye contact at a critical point in a conversation or throwing your hands into the air as you are speaking can completely contradict or overpower whatever verbal messaging you are attempting to convey. This means we must use strong emotional intelligence competencies to pay special attention to a host of nonverbal cues:

- **Eye contact.** Typically, looking someone directly in the eye when speaking to them builds trust or conveys connection. However, intense staring can also create an aggressive and uncomfortable environment.
- **Facial expressions.** Facial expressions are in many ways the window to assessing happiness, fear, anxiety, or any number of other emotional states. Being sensitive to the expressions that we carry and using our emotional intelligence skills to accurately assess the emotional state of others can go a long way in furthering communication.
- **Body language.** Body language includes our posture, our use of hands, and our nervous habits, such as tapping our fingers on the table. Slouching or turning our body away from someone else may be viewed as a sign of disinterest. Conversely, facing someone directly when speaking with them shows interest and respect.

Written Communication

Written communication includes anything we actually type or write by hand. This may include an email, a Facebook post, classroom policies, a report or memorandum, training manuals, a tweet, or a letter. The written word is a commonly used method of communication, so the ability to compose and deliver a written message is crucial in day-to-day organizational operations, especially where training and development is concerned.

Unlike verbal communication, which occurs and ends, written communication is there for all to see and assess. It can be permanent. It can be passed from person to person well into the future. The written word carries a tremendous amount of risk and power. From an emotional intelligence perspective, this places great emphasis on our ability to be aware of the impact our writing has on motivation and social dynamics. What message are we sending? We should approach what we write, how we portray our messages, and in what medium they are delivered with great care.

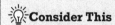
Consider This
- Which medium of communication are you most comfortable with?
- Have you ever sought assistance in preparing a message, verbal or written?
- Do you avoid a particular way of communicating (email, in person, by phone)?

Why We Struggle With Communication

From the moment we wake in the morning, we begin communicating in some measure. Sometimes we are communicating simply with ourselves; other times we're communicating with those around us. Riley and Cale, from the beginning of the chapter, were communicating in the workplace, but it can happen anywhere. And we all use multiple methods of communication: verbal, nonverbal, and written. So with all of these options, and with the act of communication being such a common occurrence, why would anyone struggle with it? Turns out there are many reasons.

Sometimes we avoid communication because we are afraid to speak up in front of others. A typical meeting, whether virtual or not, can be an intimidating experience. We may hesitate to make a point for fear of being ridiculed or judged. And things get worse if we are making our point in front of a large audience. Public speaking is a frightening endeavor. Many eyes are upon you, and people are hanging on every word you say. It's a pressure cooker. But don't feel alone. Even those who do well with speaking in public forums second-guess the clarity and impact of their message.

We also find barriers in communication when we assume, intend, and forget:

- We **assume** when we make decisions about what we think people know before we communicate with them. This affects the language we use and the data we provide. When we overestimate the effectiveness of our message before we deliver it, we are destined for problems.

- We also **intend** for our message to be well received, but that is not always the case. Think about it: Understanding intention on the part of another is a very difficult thing to do, and unless we are very clear about our message, intention will often be lost.

- Finally, we **forget**. We forget that our reality is ours, not anyone else's. Realities are affected by our childhood experiences, the way we frame an issue, even our mood. Forgetting that someone else's reality may look different from ours creates a significant communication gap.

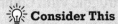
Consider This
- How many of your friends are from outside your generation?
- Which generation, other than your own, do you resonate with the most?
- Do you avoid interacting with a particular generation?

All of these barriers play a role in our ability to connect with one another. Sometimes they are driven by the way we think and perceive the world around us. Other times they may simply be physical impediments in the office, such as walls or doors. Other barriers may come in the form of organizational structure or culture. Technology contributes as well: It is all too common to find our conversations interrupted by someone checking their email.

However, there is one particular area of concern for communicating in the world today: generational barriers.

Generational Barriers

By far, one of the most fascinating dynamics occuring in the workplace is that for the first time ever, we have five generations coexisting in our organizations (Purdue University 2020). This means, for all practical purposes, that a young team member could be working with someone who is the same age as their great-grandparents. While this workforce diversity is certainly welcome, it can create communication challenges. We must therefore depend on our emotional intelligence skills to bridge the gaps. Let's look at each generation and its tendencies. Keep in mind that there are exceptions with every generation, but use this as a general guide.

- **Traditionalists** (born between 1925 and 1945). Labeled by some as the greatest generation, they saw the value of duty and sacrifice during a time of extraordinary worldwide destruction. They grew up as children being seen but not heard, and while they are fine having fun, they do so only after the hard work of the day is done. When communicating with Traditionalists, know that they value formality, authority, institutions, and an air of respectful behavior.

- **Baby Boomers** (born between 1946 and 1964). A little less formal than their Traditionalist parents, they do find value in hard work and loyalty. During conversations they tend to push back on accepted norms and ask comprehensive questions. When communicating with Boomers, remember that they are self-sufficient, confident, idealistic, and a little rebellious!

- **Generation X** (born between 1965 and 1980). This independent and resourceful generation values work–life balance. They grew up with working moms, divorced parents, and MTV. As a result, they developed self-reliance and skepticism. They are willing to leave an employer if they believe their work–life balance is at risk. When communicating with Gen X, remember they may push back if they feel overwhelmed or micromanaged.

- **Millennials** (born between 1981 and 2000). Sometimes known as Generation Y, Millennials are flexible and technologically savvy. The internet came of age at about the time Millennials were in middle school. They grew up in a connected world that included significant global disasters such as 9/11 and the 2008 financial disaster. They have a welcoming perspective toward diversity and inclusion. When communicating with Millennials, remember that they value cooperation and flexibility.

- **Gen Z** (born between 2001 and 2020). The newest addition to the workforce, Gen Z-ers are the first true digital natives. This is a generation who grew up after the internet became ubiquitous. They know nothing else. Global connection and global thinking come naturally to this generation. When communicating with Gen Z-ers, remember that their face-to-face experience with others is much more limited than in previous generations due to their digital use.

Not surprisingly, each one of these generations brings a unique perspective on everything from lifestyle to work habits to values. Boomers may prefer phone calls, but Gen Z-ers would rather text. Traditionalists may struggle with the idea of working remotely, while Millennials are comfortable working from a laptop anywhere. Having a clear understanding of the expectations of the individuals making up today's training and development population will improve not only our organizational culture, but our classrooms as well.

Improving Our Communication

With every eye upon you and people hanging on your every word, it is no wonder that communication can be daunting. Because we depend on people accurately decoding our messages, we run the risk of our messages being misconstrued. Still, we have to communicate. Every day. All the time. Pay heed to these tips and see if they help:

- **Know your audience.** This is step one every time. Knowing that your audience is multigenerational or multicultural, comes from very technical backgrounds, has lots of experience, or has a little experience is key. This will be the first guiding principle for how you craft your communication. It will help you decide the most impactful language, tone, and medium.
- **Own your nonverbal cues.** Nonverbal communication plays a huge role in the message that we send. Have someone help you by identifying nonverbal cues you may be unaware of. Many are good

and can add zest to our communication style. Others not so much. Being aware is an important step.

- **Avoid assuming, intending, and forgetting.** Remember that our intention and assumptions about our message and target audience may be completely incorrect. And our reality is only ours. Plan ahead.

- **Speak up.** Don't yell, but do project confidence in your speaking voice. If people cannot hear you, you cannot communicate your message. If you have a quiet and subtle voice, practice good speaking techniques to project and make yourself more audible. A confident tone goes a long way in spreading your message.

- **Tape yourself.** This is a terrific exercise when preparing for presentations. When we see ourselves on film, we notice our verbal and nonverbal tendencies, including using filler words (such as *um* and *like*), shifting, and fidgeting.

- **Proof your text.** Before you send out an important email, a tweet, or a learner guide for a training program, ensure that you are saying what you mean to say. The concept of a draft document that you can go back to and review has saved many a job. Have someone proofread for you. Keep your written communication simple and straightforward.

- **Save your written documents.** Sometimes after several rewrites, we end up with something that we are very proud of and that does the trick. Save these templates for future use. You never know when that beautiful prose you created could come in handy. Pulitzer Prizes await!

Practice Point—The Simple Act of Noticing!

Effective communication boils down to one common practice—the simple act of noticing—and this requires self-awareness. Imagine, for example, developing a training program with two different instructional designers. Both are knowledgeable and qualified, but you seem to connect with one better than the other, and as such, you always try to get that person assigned to your courses. Not being conscious of this, you are inadvertently setting the stage for potential workplace issues.

The first designer, Haneen, is the one you prefer. She is personable and friendly. She is well groomed and faces you directly when you meet. When she speaks, she has a pleasant tone; her language is appropriate, and not annoyingly laden with educational acronyms. Haneen pauses at the appropriate time and uses politely worded questions to ensure that you understand her advice. She also looks you in the eye while making her most salient points.

The second designer, Kevin, is the one you avoid. While technically skilled, this designer is not one that you seem to resonate with, even a little. His attire is often ruffled, his necktie askew. Kevin rarely makes eye contact, if ever, appearing instead to look directly at an object just over your left shoulder. His language is full of acronyms and lingo that he assumes you recognize. He speaks quickly, nonstop, almost as if he was in a hurry to get your meeting over with. And as he speaks, he also tends to use overly demonstrative hand gestures, which you find distracting.

No wonder you prefer Haneen! The problem lies with Kevin, who has not given any thought to the way he communicates or how he portrays his message. While this is nothing for Kevin to be ashamed of, there are many things he needs to be aware of—self-aware of, to be precise, a simple act of noticing self and others. Likewise, when we recognize our inherent bias, we are more effectively able to change our behavior through self-regulation.

Our intended message is not always received, and therein lies the major problem with communication.

A few key steps:

- Know your audience. I said this before, but it bears repeating. Before preparing for any type of communication, it is crucial to understand your audience as best you can. Be aware of their level of expertise and competence, and yours. Know what they are comfortable with, and more important, what they are uncomfortable with.

- Manage your reality. All of our realities are simply perceived realities, and we must strive to be aware of them. My reality is not your reality, and what appears right to me might look quite different to you, and even more so to a third party. Be ready in case people misperceive your message. You may need to be able to explain your ideas in a different way.

- Use the right language to connect well. You may need to adjust your language using self-regulation based on your intended audience. Be cautious of words that may be defined differently by those to whom you are presenting, especially when offering empathy. Be comfortable asking them to define a word for you so that you both remain on the same page. Avoid acronyms altogether unless you are certain your audience knows what they mean.

- Choose the right medium for your communication. It's crucial to be aware that verbal communication is not always the best solution. For that matter, neither is the written word. One will typically work better than the other, and it is important to be aware of which one is appropriate for your audience and message. Generally, longer and very detailed messages may need to be written in order to give recipients a chance to digest the material.

- Be patient with your listener. Once you've delivered your message, be ready for misunderstandings and confusion and use the proper social skills and empathetic mindset to address them. Approach these issues with an open mind and by assuming noble intent on the part of the recipient. Communication is tricky business, and sometimes we spend as much time clarifying our messages as delivering them.

Wrap-Up

Effective communication drives everything—I mean everything—in the talent development environment. When we are able to communicate well with one another, we enhance our professional capabilities, collaborate well, deliver first-class training, complete projects on time, and drive organizational success. Communication serves as the foundation for all we do.

The secrets to effective communication are not that difficult to uncover. It's all about emotional intelligence. A strong sense of self-awareness and the simple act of noticing prepares us well for being able to communicate our message—written or verbal. Whether we're speaking to a multigenerational audience or to first-time learners in a technical classroom, by being aware of our audience and sensitive to the content in our materials, we are well positioned to deliver effective development training.

As a reminder, note the role that emotional intelligence plays in the world of communication:

- Self-awareness allows us to recognize our strengths with written, verbal, and nonverbal communication. We might be good at one and need to work on the others.
- While self-regulation is not always as big of a deal for written communication, because we often have time to reconsider what we write, with nonverbal or verbal interactions it's imperative that we manage our responses in real time.
- Effective communication yields trust and a sense of being informed. This creates motivation among those in our organizations.
- As the soft, caring aspect of communications, empathy can serve to bridge gaps, bring comfort, and ease stress.
- Our social skills through written, verbal, and nonverbal communications are observed by all. Monitoring how we communicate in any form will ensure that those who witness our efforts come away with a positive vibe.

Finally, you might've noticed that I only barely touched on listening in our examination of communication. Listening matters a lot. Some communication models even include listening as a prominent component. I chose to save our exploration of listening for the next chapter, with its focus on conflict. Yes, listening matters for communication, but for conflict, it's a make or break. Read on!

CHAPTER 8
Conflict

Kelly Is Conflicted About Conflict!

Kelly has just taken a position as the new manager of technical training and talent development. She has always considered herself a people person, so when she got the opportunity to take a job where much of her work would be focused on connecting like-minded professionals, fostering relationships, and generating alignment, she was all in. As part of the new position, she had eight direct reports, and she couldn't wait to sit down with them the first time. Unfortunately, that much anticipated meeting turned out to be a disaster. People kept sniping at one another. It was obvious that there was no trust among her team. Even on the most mundane issues, they couldn't agree. Despite Kelly's most fervent attempts to lighten the mood, it wasn't happening. In the end, all but one left the room in silence. She could almost see steam rising from a few departing heads. The lone remaining supervisor, Levi, looked at her and said: "You have a problem!"

Why We Have Conflict

When we communicate well, we are able to build connections with one another. And it is those bonds that provide the foundation for potential conflict. The fact is, conflict rears its ugly head more often with the people with whom we have relationships. This can render it emotional and hurtful.

Can we have conflict with a stranger? Of course. You're standing in line at the local coffee shop and someone cuts in front of you, rudely delaying your morning dose of caffeine. You may tap them on the shoulder and say, "I'm sorry, I was here first." They may reply with, "No, you were not; I did not see you." The conversation then devolves into "Yes, I was." "No, you weren't." Conflict begins. If there is a silver lining to this type of conflict, it is that it is only temporary and you are very unlikely to see that person again. On the other hand, conflict with people we know can have a much longer-lasting impact on our relationships and the work we do.

> ☀️**Consider This**
> • When was the last time you experienced conflict with a stranger?
> • When was the last time you experienced conflict with a friend or colleague?
> • In either case, how did you feel when the conflict arose?
> • Did you react in a way that you later regretted?

Conflict is as complicated as human beings themselves. Like communication, adverse encounters involve all aspects of our emotional intelligence: self-awareness, self-regulation, motivation, empathy, and social skills. Think about what happens when we experience disagreement. Sometimes we can see it coming from a mile away. We are sitting in a meeting and someone with whom we typically differ brings up a controversial subject that you have argued about in the past. Our own personal and professional motivations come into play. We may even get a little defensive. We know what's about to happen!

When we have disagreements with others, we can generally tap into our self-awareness to recognize what we are about to feel. We may become uncomfortable and start shifting in our seats; perhaps our skin gets a little clammy or flushed, or the tone of our voice changes. We will get into how to handle this a little later in the chapter, but the fact is that we can feel conflict both physically and emotionally. It puts us off guard and affects the clarity of our thinking.

In the talent development arena, conflict may relate to differences in opinion of how workers should accomplish a particular task. For example, some may believe that the most effective way to measure learner success is through quantitative measurements. Others may consider qualitative and experiential measures to be a more accurate method. Conflict may also occur with there are differences about a particular goal. For example, should one of our goals be to recruit learners from midlevel supervisory positions for the leadership development program, or should we select learners earlier in their career? Or a stakeholder might request training to address a problem, but you don't think that training is the solution. Finally, and most often, conflict may result from differences in personalities or values.

Causes of Conflict

The underlying causes of conflict are diverse and numerous, but they apply across any industry. Regardless of profession, it is an ever-present dynamic. Let's look at some of the more common causes of conflict:

- **Perception-based conflict.** As we learned in the previous chapter, perception matters. An improperly placed comma or the use of all caps in an email or an insensitive tone in conversation may cause perception problems that lead to conflict.
- **Role-based conflict.** It is not uncommon in today's busy talent development world for team members to do work that's not normally part of their daily job. Conflict is sure to follow if we are asked to step outside our comfort zones or paygrade to accomplish tasks.
- **Resource-based conflict.** We never seem to have enough resources to complete our jobs. There will always be tools, techniques, and equipment that help us deliver our training mission, but fewer dollars to pay for them than we would like. When competition for resources contributes to failure of our instructional and educational mission, conflict is likely to occur.
- **Pressure-based conflict.** Fewer resources and confusion about who is responsible for what, combined with a hectic training environment, can also lead to pressure-based conflict. This can

be exacerbated by other types of anxiety as well, including emotional, performance, or peer pressure.

- **Style-based conflict.** We all have communication and leadership styles that we are more comfortable with. Unfortunately, different styles do not always mesh well together. Working individually, we are not often faced with style conflict. However, when working in teams, conflicting styles occur often.
- **Motivation-based conflict.** Self-awareness requires that we own our personal and professional motivations. On the positive side, motivation gives us direction and focus; however, when used for personal gain, motivation can create problems, especially in times of conflict.
- **Power-based conflict.** At some point in all of our work relationships, we find ourselves in the position of needing to exercise power, or of being the target of someone else's power. Power is something we all have and use. When two types of power intersect, well, you know the rest.

The Price We Pay for Conflict Avoidance

We shouldn't be too hard on ourselves when we acknowledge that we have trouble with conflict, and that we avoid it. It is a perfectly natural human attribute to seek harmony and acceptance. Honestly, it is so much more pleasant to go through life without having to deal with conflict at a personal or professional level. And given the impact conflict has on us, it's no wonder we often avoid it.

Ask yourself these questions:

- Did I grow up in a home that avoided conflict at all costs?
- Do I worry about being liked?
- Am I willing to be a martyr just to avoid a fight?
- Do I skillfully redirect conversations when conflict occurs?
- Do I keep a scorecard of unresolved conflicts?

If you answered yes to three or more of these, you may be allergic to conflict. You're not alone. Many in our workplace go to great lengths to avoid negative encounters. In fact, research suggests that up to 95 percent of people avoid conflict with their co-workers, costing organizations immensely in the process (Vansyckle 2018).

Many people avoid conflict because it creates an intense amount of uncertainty, discomfort, and anxiety. Conflict activates our fight-or-flight self-protection mechanism, causing many of us to feel clammy and overadrenalized. We may physically tremble, our voices may rise, and more often than not, we say things we regret later. Feelings get hurt and relationships damaged. It is no wonder many of us shy away from conflict. Even if we have strong self-awareness, and are aware that disagreement is about to occur, we tend to have these unpleasant physical reactions. It is not a comfortable thing! We may also have emotional reactions—sadness, depression, anxiety. Finally, being unable to control our reactions to conflict through self-regulation can lead to feelings of despair or fear when confronted with conflict.

Other, more deep-seated reasons for circumventing battles exist as well. Conflict avoidance can be traced back to many people's childhoods. Some grew up in environments where conflict was common, while others grew up in families that did everything they could to minimize disagreement. Previous experience also comes into play if we were involved in a significant conflict that was especially harmful. Our desire to protect ourselves may lead us to avoid conflict in the future based on this one occasion. Rather than constructively engaging in conflict, we find ourselves shutting down. It just feels safer.

We may also be conflict-averse because we value relationships with others, especially if we are people pleasers by nature. Working relationships are difficult enough. We may choose to avoid conflict simply because we do not want to hurt someone else's feelings. Many is the time that we sidestep a difficult situation for fear of making things problematic for someone else. Similarly, where work relationships are concerned, we may fear being ridiculed or rejected by other professionals on whom we depend. Any internal uncertainty exacerbates these conditions and causes us to dodge conflict no matter the cost.

Lastly, we avoid conflict because of our own uncertainty. When we are not confident in our abilities, or when we fear that our opinion won't be welcomed, it is easy for us to slip into a neurologically protective stance. We may not think we have the skills to address whatever situation has revealed itself to us, and we don't take the risk of sharing an opinion no matter how valid it is. We slip into a cocoon of safety and protect ourselves from potential disappointment.

The impact of unresolved conflict on the workplace can be extreme. In the most comprehensive study of workplace conflict in the last 20 years, researchers estimated the cost of conflict to be $359 billion annually (CPP 2008). Not surprisingly, this cost reflects a working environment where conflict is pervasive. The study also found that:

- 85 percent of employees deal with some conflict.
- 29 percent of employees deal with conflict constantly.
- 49 percent of conflict is a result of ego and personality.
- 34 percent of conflict occurs among frontline employees.
- 34 percent of conflict is caused by stress in the workplace.
- 33 percent of conflict is caused by heavy workloads.
- 27 percent of employees have witnessed conflicts that escalated to personal attacks.
- 25 percent of employees have seen conflict result in sickness or missed work.

These numbers are sobering indeed. The inability to deal with conflict in an organization can wreak havoc on the health and performance of employees no matter the industry. Those who work in environments of excessive conflict struggle with any number of physical or emotional responses, such as headaches, problems sleeping, or even eating disorders. Workplace absenteeism and turnover become the new normal. Motivation and morale plummet. Performance suffers as individuals spend more time navigating a toxic organizational culture and less time making sound strategic decisions to enhance the mission of the organization.

What is potentially worse for our talent development world is not so much the conflict that we face or even the impact the conflict has. What may matter more than anything is the amount of conflict debt that is present in our workplace. Liane Davey, in her 2019 book, *The Good Fight: Use Productive Conflict to Get Your Team and Organization Back on Track*, introduces the concept of conflict debt as the sum of all the touchy matters that need to be addressed in organizations but remain unresolved. As issues occur, we decide to put them on the back burner. We convince ourselves that we have a good reason to do so—we're busy, the end of the fiscal year is near, a training session is about to start. Still, these issues sit, gaining momentum and importance, as we ignore them in favor of other more easily accomplished tasks. As conflict debt accumulates, the resources necessary to deal with it become almost unattainable.

The lesson? Don't let conflict go unresolved.

Yet we do. According to Davey, we tend to react by avoiding conflict, avoiding the opposition, or avoiding friction. We avoid conflict by focusing on things that we think are more important at the time (or, if we're being completely honest with ourselves, anything at all that can keep our minds off the conflict). We avoid the opposition by pushing away those with whom we disagree and surrounding ourselves with those who see the world through our lens. We avoid friction by not discussing all aspects of the conflict. In other words, when the conversation gets difficult, we back away, perhaps putting it in the proverbial parking lot for later discussion. And of course, we never return to it, and thus our conflict debt grows.

☀ Consider This

- How does your organization deal with conflict?
- Are you able to list three or more areas where your organization is in conflict debt?
- What is the current state of action for each of those areas?

When Conflict Is Positive

If there is one single interpersonal dynamic where we can exercise our emotional intelligence skills the most, it would be in the presence of conflict. Conflict allows us to tap into our own self-awareness, recognizing a disagreement as it arrives on the landscape. It also fosters self-regulation skills that are absolutely critical for us to make conflict a positive situation. We must take those emotional forces and translate them into constructive actions: a soft and understanding voice. Eye contact. Appropriate non-verbal communication. When taken together, they can create a positive outcome for conflict, instead of a negative one.

When we are able to use our emotional intelligence competencies in pursuit of positive conflict, we also enjoy the added benefit of building relationships. Having a welcoming perspective on conflict allows team members to say what they want, and what they think. This is an enormously beneficial attribute for organizations. Positive conflict also has the ability to open new avenues of discussion. By bouncing ideas off one another and using our emotional intelligence skills to recognize and value the input of our colleagues, we are able to measure our own views against those of others. We are able to incrementally build on our thoughts, and couple them with those of others, to make better and more informed decisions.

Not surprisingly, organizations benefit greatly when positive conflict is nurtured. Trusting and positive work relationships lead to better performance and productivity across the board. But these relationships are not limited to person to person. Divisions and departments build trust with one another on a more comprehensive scale because of the individual interactions of the people within. And when cross-functional teams work better together, before you know it, there is a culture of healthy trust and respect among all.

Improving Our Conflict Management

Conflict may appear to be one of the more difficult dynamics to face either personally or organizationally. Disagreements among those with whom we work run the risk of creating fissures in our organizations that are difficult to overcome. And make no mistake, conflict will always be there. It is up to us to make it a positive event that fosters organizational growth and success, rather than a negative one that can spell disaster. To make conflict work for us, consider the following steps:

- **Have an open mind.** It takes extraordinary self-awareness to admit when we are not entering a conflict situation with an open mind. Given our emotionally laden souls, it's not surprising, but it does create problems. Any predetermined blame, assessment, or opinion may be all that is necessary to doom the discussion.

- **Own your stuff.** We all enter into or avoid conflict with our own baggage. Sometimes it is the "I'm not good enough to be here" baggage, so we do everything we can to avoid conflict. Sometimes it is the "I must prove myself to others" baggage, so we take the necessary steps, fair and unfair, to win. Neither of these approaches works. Be aware of what you're carrying before trying to tackle any conflict.

- **Have a plan.** Think about what you want to achieve before the conflict develops. When entering a situation where conflict may occur, decide exactly what your message needs to be. Write it down so it is easier to remember. Think about how you might deliver this message in a way that would foster cooperation and not consternation (see the previous chapter). Remember, relationships matter, and poisoning them rarely results in long-term success.

- **Take personal interests out of it.** Try to focus on mutual interests and measurable outcomes. Once you can reach agreement on what you're trying to accomplish, it becomes much easier to forge a path to get there. Agreement begets agreement, and a little time invested in an unemotional conversation about mutual interests may be all you need to avoid significant conflict.

- **Find comfort with comfort.** One of the great tools in handling conflict is being empathetic to the needs and concerns of another person. When we are able to implement this critical emotional intelligence skill, we can soothe past wounds and build future partnerships.

- **Ask for what you need (and feel free to say no).** We are typically not very good about asking for what we need. We like the idea of being self-sufficient, and asking for something makes us feel weak. However, polite and firm conversations about what we are willing to do, not do, and need helps to build a foundation of trust and respect.

- **Build a culture of trust.** You might notice that this is a recurring theme in this book. Trust can never be underestimated. Look for ways to build constructive conflict that is open, honest, and excepting. Courtesy and kindness matter. When we are able to have productive, constructive discussions, we foster a commitment for our organization that yields benefits far down the line.

- **Reflect, reflect, reflect.** Give careful thought to your experience with conflict afterward. Think through how you conducted yourself, what you said, and most important, what you meant. Keep a journal, think about ways to improve, and practice them the next time around. Conflict will always be present, so you'll have plenty of opportunity.

Practice Point—Listen!

Think about the last time you were in a conversation where you thought people weren't listening to you. How did it feel? Chances are, you came away from that conversation feeling less than appreciated. Perhaps you believed the other person was less than engaged with you. Perhaps your assessment was that they didn't really care about you or your issue.

Now, layer conflict on top of this conversation. Emotions were high. You were concerned about resources, project success, your professional reputation, and the like. The problem is that the other person in the conversation likely felt the same way, which may have been one of the reasons that they were not listening very well. They were more interested in their own position. Regardless, that conversation probably didn't go very well. Bad listening made a bad situation even worse.

When we insert strong emotional intelligence competencies into the listening equation, we create an environment where people believe their message is being taken seriously. They feel cared for. If we begin by recognizing whether or not we are a good listener, we set the stage for success. By self-regulating our desire to interrupt someone midsentence, we create a new environment for open communication and conflict resolution. When we listen empathetically, we exude the message that we think the person we are listening to is important. Likewise, if our conversation is being witnessed by others, it sets an example for respectful and open communication for all to see.

Now think about a conversation that you had when you were truly listened to. Perhaps it was with a mentor, and you were sharing your concerns about and plans for your talent development future. You were looking for advice and guidance. More than likely, if the mentor was a good listener, you came away from the conversation feeling cared for and valued. Even if we were to add conflict to this dynamic, a good listener creates a foundation for a real connection when communicating, and their patience and skill lessen the likelihood of unconstructive conflict occurring.

Bad listening has been referred to as the common cold of leadership, but it infects all organizational levels. Listening is an exceptionally difficult skill to build, but it yields benefits beyond belief. Good listeners have a calm, patient presence. They don't think about what they are going to say while you are speaking. They simply listen intently, actively, and empathetically. It is a skill crucial to our success.

A few key steps:

- Set yourself up for listening success by having a conversation in the proper environment. Many open-office settings do not provide the appropriate amount of privacy for difficult conversations. Do your best to speak in an area where you will not be interrupted.

If the conversation is a virtual one, stay focused on the screen and refrain from too much movement that would pull you away from your focus on the individual. Leave your cell phone in another room and turn off other computer notifications.

- Be patient. Not everyone communicates in the same way you do. Some may stumble over their words, become emotional, or even forget what they wanted to say. And, even though we think we may be able to say it better than what we're hearing, that is not our job at the moment. Give the speaker the patience and empathy you would expect for yourself.
- Use this newfound patience to listen with your whole being. Empathy matters here. When we listen thoughtfully, we listen to speech, nonverbal cues, and what's not said. Speakers communicate with their entire bodies. We should listen with our entire body. Be present.
- Don't feel like you have to solve the problem. You don't. And if you do try to solve the problem, you probably will be thinking about what you want to say while you are supposed to be listening. Sometimes listening is just listening, and the real purpose of a conversation is for someone to get something off their chest.
- Understand your own motivations before, during, and after listening. By being self-aware about where we stand on a given issue, we are better able to hear the true message of those with whom we communicate.
- Remember that listening works for conflict situations. During disagreements, listening can create the silence and space necessary to calm the nerves and keep the conversation balanced. However, the power of listening goes well beyond conflict. It enhances every aspect of organizational life.

The next time you're dealing with a stubborn subject matter expert who wants to include too much content in a training course, a manager who won't make time for their direct reports to attend your learning program, or another designer who isn't meeting your quality expectations, use these tips.

Wrap-Up

Conflict is present in all aspects of our professional lives, whether it's communication, discussions of organizational strategy, or decisions about our own professional capabilities. Historically, we view such conflicts as negative. We dread them. We consider them something to avoid. When they are handled poorly, this is indeed the case. Conflict can create tension that can lead to significant physical and emotional challenges. Conflict can also generate an organizational climate that doesn't meet performance objectives. But all is not lost.

Note the role that emotional intelligence plays in the world of conflict:

- Self-awareness allows us to own where we stand on the issue of conflict. Is it something we welcome? Is it something we fear? Is it something we pursue?
- Self-regulation gives us the ability to recognize our triggers so that during conflict, we are able to keep the conversation positive and moving forward.
- Through self-awareness, we can better understand what motivates us and others. This gives us the common ground for solutions to even the most vexing organizational problems.
- Empathy is the ultimate comfort food for conflict. By exhibiting authentic empathy, we draw people toward us in an effort to mutually resolve disagreements.
- Social skills can play a huge role, especially when emotions start to rise during times of conflict. Remember, we are always being watched and judged by those around us. Keeping calm and dignified during conflict deescalates matters and positions us for more fruitful discussions.

Conflict is not a bad thing. When viewed through a more positive lens, it can go a long way toward enhancing innovation and imagination among our colleagues. By using emotional intelligence, we can build a foundation for positive conflict both personally and organizationally. The synergy created in places where we work is reflective of an open and exciting environment of discussion, disagreement, and innovative solutions. Embrace conflict! Keep it positive and watch it work for you.

CHAPTER 9

Where to Go From Here

My Appeal to You

We've likely never met in person or virtually, so it may seem unusual for this final chapter to begin with such a personal and direct petition. It may even seem out of place in an ATD professional series. However, our use of emotional intelligence transcends formality. It trumps all the tips, tricks, and processes that we've been taught as we've grown in our talent development careers. It's not that the technical components of our work are unimportant. They are crucial. They give us the tools to deliver first-rate training and position our learners for maximum success. But they are not enough. When we lean on these instructional strategies without a foundation of emotional well-being, we will never have the impact on our learners and our organizations that we could potentially have.

We began this journey many chapters ago with our exploration of the components of emotional intelligence, and we have traced the use of emotional intelligence competencies through our exploration of stress, multitasking, communication, and conflict. And as much as it would be pleasing for you to see this as the be-all and end-all to the exploration and use of emotional intelligence in the work of a talent development professional, that is simply not the case. The intent of the previous chapters was to stitch these concepts of emotional intelligence together with a practical application in the workplace—and in life.

Where do we go from here? It would be so easy to nod, send me an email telling me how much you enjoy the book, and move on to the next task at hand. But that would be a disappointing ending to the journey we have taken together on this all-important topic of emotional intelligence. So how do we apply the concepts presented in this book now and in the future? Is there a way for us to use emotional intelligence as a foundation for the way we live our life and the way we practice our trade? Can we do more? The answer is yes.

As you will recall from the first three chapters of the book, emotional intelligence entails an appreciation of self-awareness, self-regulation, motivation, empathy, and social skills. Few, if any, concepts are so directly related to our happiness and our success. Self-awareness allows us to recognize who we really are, the good and the bad. It gives us a foundation of authenticity. Self-regulation provides the ability to calm ourselves in the event of emotional hijack. We are effectively able to moderate our behavior and not let our emotions get the best of us. Understanding our motivation helps us be clear about what gets us up in the morning, gets us to work, and keeps us happy. Empathy bridges the gap with others, and our social skills serve as our radar for the unique needs of all individuals. Mastering these competencies, and growing while we do, allows us to better understand ourselves and others, and they serve as a foundation for success in work, and especially in life.

Following the path of emotional intelligence is fraught with challenges. Doing the hard work to make ourselves more aware of the way we think and how we perceive others takes humility and commitment. When done well, embracing the tenets of self-awareness, self-regulation, empathy, motivation, and social skills makes us better talent development professionals, and better people. It's a journey, though. It is not as simple as reading a book, checking off a few list items, and considering your mission accomplished. And that path to success begins with setting realistic goals, building your support system, and tracking your success.

Set Realistic Goals

I know how it feels to be so excited to apply a new concept that you go forth with reckless abandon. It's an exciting time and one worth relishing. Personally, I tend to be a little overly enthusiastic. At this very moment, my friends are reading this and laughing while they utter, "Yeah, Patrick, ya think?" It is true. I tend to think very positively and see the bright side no matter what situation I'm in. Call it the power of positive thinking, call it being Pollyannaish, call it sunshine. Whatever it is, I have it. For some reason, my default position is that if we can just find the positive in any situation we're in, we'll be better off.

If this describes you, don't be ashamed. According to scientists, there are many of us! It turns out that people have a remarkable ability to hold a positive outlook on any number of topics. In fact, we are far more likely to overemphasize the positive and underestimate the negative. From work to our personal life to our physical and emotional health, we always seem to think positive, convincing ourselves we have a better than average chance at success and happiness. Scientists call this optimism bias (Sharot 2011).

I like the idea that we are positive by nature, that we look for the good in others, and that we hope for the best for ourselves and those we care about. However, there is a very strong case to be made for setting realistic goals, even if we stay positive along the way. Setting realistic goals gives us the best chance for celebrating our success, not getting too down when things don't go the way we had hoped, and ensuring long-term happiness. Let's call it being a positive realist.

What are some of the best ways to be a positive realist? First, remember that life is not always fair. In the event that things don't go our way, one measure of comfort is the fact that life doesn't always go anyone's way every time. Some people may appear to get all the breaks, but this is unlikely to be actually true. Life is life, no matter who we are. Many people find joy even in the most extreme circumstances. Perhaps when we look at ourselves and what we have, we'll find that life is not so bad after all, even with the occasional unwanted outcome.

Second, when setting goals and preparing to move up to that next talent development position, remember that it is important to exercise honest self-awareness of what you may face along the path. Perhaps you are not ready for a particular position at this point. Perhaps a little more experience will do the trick. Or maybe that job just isn't the right fit for you. Be honest with yourself and give yourself the best opportunity for the best decision.

Third, a positive realist also knows that bad things may happen. When they do, we must find the resilience to move forward. Remember that resilience is often associated with bucking up and being stronger. But that is a faulty definition. In truth, resilience is all about self-care. When things don't go our way, self-care is our first act. Then we regroup and reassess the situation, looking at what lessons may be available and what new paths may have opened for us.

Build Your Support System

Humans need humans. Relationships give us strength; help us lead healthier, longer lives; and have more success at every level. One of the broken traditional values of our culture is the "pull yourself up by your bootstraps" mentality, which is the foundation of the individualist origin of our nation. Certainly, individual liberties and justice are important, as is personal motivation and character. But thinking that we have to live our lives and pursue our career goals alone is an unfortunate perspective, and one that has the potential to leave us alone and wanting.

Why would we ever not lean on others? I don't have an answer for this. We should depend on others, and we should do it often. Friends, family, and colleagues are endless sources of advice and guidance. They support us when we need it. They also provide a valuable outside perspective, no matter what our struggles. When we are able to depend on others, we have a sense of comfort and safety that allows us to be creative and take risks. Our self-esteem is boosted. We feel better about what we do, and we are more likely to reach out and help others as well.

Think for a moment about the last time you bombed in a classroom. It happens to all of us! And sometimes, all we want is to share that experience with someone else. It feels good to talk about it and get it off our chest. We don't always need answers or advice; sometimes we just need emotional support. We need to know that someone else finds us valuable and that these days will come and go. We simply cannot put a price on this type of dynamic. We benefit emotionally by feeling cared for and loved. We benefit physically through reduced anxiety and lower blood pressure. We also benefit intellectually. When we have someone with whom we feel safe to share items of concern, we open our mind for potential new solutions.

My dear friend and colleague Bob Tobias of American University had what I thought was a very unusual practice when he would interview graduate students or federal executives for placement in his program. He would always end the interview by asking them, "What do you need from me to be successful in this program?" The answers that potential students gave were always along the lines of how much they appreciate getting the readings in advance, having someone available for questions about the content, or having a flexible schedule as they pursue their educational goals. But this is not what Bob meant. What he was looking for was for the potential student to tell him what they needed from him. In other words, he wanted them to ask him for something. In only the rarest of cases did this actually happen.

The reason that this rarely occurred in those interviews was because we have a hard time asking for what we need, whether from a colleague, an employer, a friend, or a relative. We don't want to appear weak. We are all about self-preservation. We also don't want to put anyone in a difficult position. And sometimes, our pride factor is a little too high. It is a bit of a humility test, truth be told. When we ask for what we need, we show vulnerability.

We could all benefit from recognizing that we have needs. Sometimes these desires are very personal. Sometimes it's as simple as professional advice. But they are needs, nonetheless. Unmet, they create gaps in our thinking. We may suffer emotionally when we fail to ask for what we need.

Seek help. Accept help. Set up regular times to meet with colleagues, friends, and family. (It is perfectly fine for some of these events to be just for fun.) Reach out to those that you need in order to be successful in life and in your career. Let them help you, and be there to help them. In much the same way that communication begets communication, kindness begets kindness. When others help us, we are more likely to help others. And so the story goes, the fabric builds, and we all become better people.

Track Your Success

OK, this is the part where I try to trip you up. I know I waited until the very end of the book to do so, but I figured if I did it earlier, you'd probably throw the book away. By now, you've committed the time and attention to this work, so I hope you don't mind. Thank you for playing along!

There are two keywords in this section: track and success. Let's be honest. Tracking is no big deal. There are a number of tools that we can use to track our success: journals, smartphones, laptops, tablets, day-timers (for those of you that remember those), and simple pen and paper. The method really doesn't matter here—whatever makes it easiest for you to capture your thoughts and track your achievements toward your success. Do what works for you.

And here comes the trick. Success: What does this mean?

It may seem that we're looking at success solely through a professional lens. But that is not the case. Let me explain with a personal story. Early in my career as a naval officer, an admiral asked me where I saw myself in 10 years. I always hated that question. How in the world would I know where I'd be in 10 years? I knew what the admiral was looking for. He wanted me to tell him that I saw myself in a position with a title, a rank, and lots of responsibility. The admiral wasn't looking for where

I saw myself in 10 years. He wanted me to tell him what job I wanted to hold 10 years down the line. See the difference?

This got me thinking about what success really meant. Is success a title or a position in an organization? Sure, that may be part of it, and it probably should be. It is a blessing beyond belief to be in a profession where we can aspire to do great things and make a difference in people's lives. Having professional goals or aspirations and seeking meaningful work is nothing to be ashamed of. But is it the only measure of success?

As you track your success over the course of your career, please keep in mind the broad meaning of the word. Is success something deeper? Something beyond what you do at work? Perhaps success is simply being emotionally healthy, balanced, and content with your life. Maybe it involves the appreciation of the simpler aspects of our time here on Earth, like enjoying a sunset, a taco, or the adoring smile of a grandchild. Being a person of character, authenticity, and integrity may also be considered a measure of success. Maybe it's simply caring for others, showing empathy and compassion, fighting for justice, and exhibiting an undying passion for human good.

A Final Thought

Let's return to where we started. In the introduction, we examined a table that had several emotions listed, and you were asked following three questions. Try answering them again, and observe how your responses have changed.

1. Which of these emotions describes where you spend the majority of your time?

_____

_____

2. Which of these emotions do you fear the most?

_____

_____

3. Which of these emotions do you wish you could feel more?

_____

_____

If you have taken one step closer to being able to answer these questions in an authentic and vulnerable way, congratulations! It is not an easy thing to do. Owning our own emotions and recognizing those in others is a powerful way to bridge the gap in communication not only in the workplace but in our personal lives as well. And it's not easy.

This book was written for professionals who build and nurture the talent and skills of others. Whether you serve as an instructional systems designer, a faculty member, or staff support, you make a difference in the worlds of those whose lives you touch. A little self-awareness here and there, with a little self-regulation, empathy, motivation, and the simple act of noticing, is a strong foundation for the work that you do.

It is my most humble hope that what we've shared in this book will be something you can use to enhance your emotional intelligence not only in the classroom, but outside the classroom, in the communities where you live and with the people you love. My final appeal to you is to use the content in this book to leave everyone you meet feeling better about themselves, and everywhere you go a better place.

Peace.
Patrick

References

Almeida, D.M., S.T. Charles, J. Mogle, J. Drewelies, C.M. Aldwin, A. Spiro III, and D. Gerstorf. 2020. "Charting Adult Development Through (Historically Changing) Daily Stress Processes." *American Psychologist* 75(4): 511–24. doi.org/10.1037/amp0000597.

American Institute of Stress. 2020. "Workplace Stress." stress.org /workplace-stress.

APA (American Psychological Association). 2020. "Stress in America." Press release, American Psychological Association. apa.org/news /press/releases/stress/2020/report.

Bader, C., J. Baker, L. Day, and A. Gordon. 2020. *Fear Itself: The Causes and Consequences of Fear in America.* New York: New York University Press.

Bar-On, R. 2006. "The Bar-On Model of Emotional-Social Intelligence (ESI)." *Psicothema* 18 (suppl.): 13–25.

Beaton, C. 2017. "The Millennial Workforce: How Multitasking Is Changing Our Brains." *Forbes,* January 27. forbes.com/sites /carolinebeaton/2017/01/27/the-millennial-workforce-how -multitasking-is-changing-our-brains/?sh=4d61b7923605.

Bennis, W. 2004. "The Crucibles of Authentic Leadership." In *The Nature of Leadership,* edited by J. Antonakis, A.T. Cianciolo, and R.J. Sternberg, 331–42. Thousand Oaks, CA: Sage Publications.

Boyatzis, R., and M. Burckle. 1999. *Psychometric Properties of the ECI.* Boston: Hay/McBer Group.

Chandler, M. 2019. "LinkedIn Global Talent Trends." LinkedIn Talent Solutions. business.linkedin.com/content/dam/me/business/en-us /talent-solutions/resources/pdfs/global-talent-trends-2019.pdf.

Cohen, S., T. Kamarck, and R. Mermelstein. 1983. "A Global Measure of Perceived Stress." *Journal of Health and Social Behavior* 24:386–96.

Covey, S. 2020. *The Seven Habits of Highly Effective People*. New York: Simon and Schuster.

CPP. 2008. "Workplace Conflict and How Businesses Can Harness It to Thrive." CPP, July. themyersbriggs.com/download/item /f39a8b7fb4fe4daface552d9f485c825.

Davey, L. 2019. *The Good Fight: Use Productive Conflict to Get Your Team and Organization Back on Track*. Vancouver: Page Two Books.

Deloitte. 2017. "Soft Skills for Business Success." deakinco.com/uploads /Whitepaper/deloitte-au-economics-deakin-soft-skills-business -success-170517.pdf.

Godin, S. 2017. "Let's Stop Calling Them 'Soft Skills'." itsyourturnblog .com/lets-stop-calling-them-soft-skills-9cc27ec09ecb.

Goleman, D. 1995. *Emotional Intelligence: Why It Can Matter More Than IQ*. New York: Bantam.

———. 1998. *Working With Emotional Intelligence*. New York: Bantam.

———. 2004. "What Makes a Leader?" *Best of HBR 1998*. Harvard Business Review: January.

Goleman, D., R. Boyatzis, and A. McKee. 2013. *Primal Leadership: Unleashing the Power of Emotional Intelligence*. Brighton, MA: Harvard Business Review Press.

Hammond, C. 2016. "Why Your Brain Likes It When You Multi-Task." BBC Future, February 19. bbc.com/future/article/20160218-why -multi-tasking-might-not-be-such-a-bad-idea.

Kahneman, D. 2011. *Thinking, Fast and Slow*. New York: Farrar, Straus and Giroux.

Kegan, R., and L. Lahey. 2017. *Immunity to Change: How to Overcome It and Unlock the Potential in Yourself and Your Organization*. Brighton, MA: Harvard Business Review Press.

Lea, R., S. Davis, B. Mahoney, and P. Qualter. 2019. "Does Emotional Intelligence Buffer the Effects of Acute Stress? A Systematic Review." *Frontiers of Psychology* April. doi.org/10.3389/fpsyg.2019.00810.

Lecic-Tosevski D., and J. Vukovic. 2011. "Stress and Personality." *Psychiatriki* 22(4): 290–97.

Leroy, S. 2009. "Why Is It So Hard to Do My Work? The Challenge of Attention Residue When Switching Between Work Tasks." *Organizational Behavior and Human Decision Processes* 109(2): 168–81.

MacKay, J. 2018. "Communication Overload." *Rescue Time*, July 11. blog. rescuetime.com/communication-multitasking-switches.

———. 2019. "Context Switching Can Kill Up to 80% of Your Productive Time." *Rescue Time*, May 30. blog.rescuetime.com/context-switching.

Mayo Clinic Staff. 2020. "Positive Thinking: Stop Negative Self-Talk to Reduce Stress." Mayo Clinic, January 21. mayoclinic.org/healthy -lifestyle/stress-management/in-depth/positive-thinking /art-20043950.

Palmer, P. 1999. *Let Your Life Speak: Listening for the Voice of Vocation.* San Francisco: Jossey-Bass.

Purdue University. 2020. "Generational Differences in the Workplace." Purdue University. purdueglobal.edu/education-partnerships /generational-workforce-differences-infographic.

Sharot, T. 2011. "The Optimism Bias." *Current Biology* 21(23): R941–45.

Six Seconds. 2018. *State of the Heart 2018.* Six Seconds. 6seconds.org /2018/09/05/state-of-the-heart-2018.

Smith, D. 2020. "Nonverbal Communication: How Body Language & Nonverbal Cues Are Key." *Lifesize*, February 18. lifesize.com/en /video-conferencing-blog/speaking-without-words.

Steinhorst, C. 2020. "How To Reclaim The Huge Losses That Multi-tasking Forces On Your Company." *Forbes*, February 28. forbes.com /sites/curtsteinhorst/2020/02/28/how-to-reclaim-the-huge-losses-that-multitasking-forces-on-your-companwy/?sh=2ee1f566c024.

Sundem, G. 2012. "This Is Your Brain on Multitasking." *Psychology Today*, February 24. psychologytoday.com/us/blog/brain-trust/201202 /is-your-brain-multitasking.

Uncapher, M., and A. Wagner. 2018. "Minds and Brains of Media Multitaskers: Current Findings and Future Directions." *Proceedings of the National Academy of Sciences of the United States of America* (*PNAS*) 115(40): 9889–96.

Vansyckle, J. 2018. "The Cost of Conflict Avoidance." Thrive Global, August 22. thriveglobal.com/stories/the-cost-of-conflict-avoidance.

Watson, J., and D. Strayer. 2010. "Supertaskers: Profiles in Extraordinary Multitasking Ability." *Psychonomic Bulletin & Review* 17:479–85.

Whiting, K.,2020. "Top Ten Skills of 2025: the 4 Trends Transforming Your Workplace." World Economic Forum. weforum.org/agenda/2020/10 /top-10-work-skills-of-tomorrow-how-long-it-takes-to-learn-them/

Wilson, K. and J.H. Korn. 2007. "Attention During Lectures: Beyond Ten Minutes." *Teaching of Psychology* 34(2): 85–89.

Index

Page numbers followed by *f* refer to figures.

A

absenteeism, 42–43, 74, 92
acute stress, 45–46
affective intelligence, 4
agreement, 95
American Institute of Stress, 43
American Psychological Association
    (APA), 42
American University, ix, 105
amygdala hijacking, 8
analysis paralysis, 51
Angelou, Maya, 3
anxiety
    and multitasking, 60, 65
    personality traits and, 51–53
    and stress, 39, 43
APA (American Psychological Association), 42
approval seeking, 22
assumptions, 30, 79–80, 83
attention residue, 64–67, 69
attention span, 67
attentive listening, 9
audience, knowing your, 82, 84, 86
authenticity, 3
authority, positional, ix
avoidance
    communication, 79
    conflict, 90–93

B

Baby Boomers, 81, 82
bad stress, 45
"baggage," owning your, 95
barriers to emotional intelligence, 21–31
    fear as, 24–26
    internal and subconscious, 21
    in organizations, 26–27
    stage of mind as, 21–23
    taking action to overcome, 28–30
    thinking patterns as, 23–24
The Beatles, ix
Bennis, Warren, 30
bias, 21, 84, 103
Binet, Alfred, 12
body language, 78
bonding, 28, 35–36
Bradberry, Travis, 4
breaks, taking, 69
Broca, Paul, 11
the Buddha, 17
burnout, 16, 39, 42

C

calendars, 70–71
career advancement, 16
caring, stress from, 52
cell phones, 60–61, 68
certainty, desire for, 28

change
    in organizations, 27
    resistance to, 52–53
    in talent development, 35–36
Chapman University, 25
chronic stress, 45–46
clarifying questions, 77
climate. *See* culture, organizational
cognitive capacity, 12
comfort, with conflict, 95–96
communication, 73–86
    case example, 73
    in conflict, 89, 90, 94
    forms of, 76–79, 85
    listening in, 96–99
    methods of improving, 82–83
    noticing in, 83–85
    in organizations, 15–16
    reasons for difficulties in, 79–82
    self-awareness about, 6
    and social skills, 11
    and stress, 58
    by TD professionals, 39
    in workplace, 73–76
communication skills, assessing, 75–76
concentration, 54, 66
confidence, 6, 24, 83, 92
conflict, 87–100
    avoiding, 90–93
    case example, 87
    causes of, 89–90
    listening during, 96–99
    positive, 94
    reasons for, 87–89
    for TD professionals, 39
conflict debt, 93
conflict management, 16, 94–96
connection(s), ix–x
    and conflict, 87, 88
    emotional intelligence to build, 5, 14
    and empathy, 9
    language for, 85
    in organizations, 16

context switching, 63–64
controlling leadership style, 4
coping, 14, 49, 53
Covey, Stephen, 8
COVID-19 pandemic, 43
credentials, viii
crucibles, 29–30
culture, organizational, 27, 74, 94, 96

D

Davey, Linda, 93
day-timer planner, 70
debt, conflict, 93
decision making, 8, 14, 23, 51
delayed return environments, 50–51
depression, 14, 43
diet, multitasking and, 65
direct address, of stressors, 55–57
diversity, workforce, 80–82
doubt, 26
driving, cell phone use while, 68

E

economic sources of stress, 43
ego, 26, 73, 92
EI. *See* emotional intelligence
email, checking, 42, 60, 63, 69
emotional intelligence (EI). *See also* barriers to emotional intelligence
    applications of, 101–108
    benefits of, for TD professionals, x, 35–36
    case example, vii–viii, x
    defined, 4–6
    domains of, 6–11
    and expertise, 3
    history of, 3–4
    individual benefits of, 13–15
    IQ and EQ, 11–12
    mindfulness and, 17
    organizational benefits of, 15–17
    reasons for overlooking, viii–x

"Emotional Intelligence" (Salovey and Mayer), 4
emotions
    during conflict, 91
    effect of stress on, 54
    self-awareness of, 6–8
    shared, 9–10
emotions exercise, xii–xiii, 107–108
empathy, 3, 9–10
    in communication, 74, 86
    during conflict, 95–96, 99
    happiness and success from, 102
    listening with, 97, 98
    mindfulness to increase, 17
    and multitasking, 72
    and stress, 52, 58
    for TD professionals, 40
    and vulnerability, 28–29
employee assistance programs, 54
environment
    for listening, 97–98
    productivity and, 66–68
EQ measure, 11–12, 14
events, stress-causing, 45–46, 50
exhaustion, 59, 60
expertise, 3, 25
extrinsic drives, 8–9
eye contact, 78

F

FaceTime, 77
face-to-face communication, 82
facial expressions, 78
fear
    of change, 52–53
    as EI barrier, 24–26, 28
    of public speaking, 79
feedback, 7
feelings, connecting with, 29
fight-or-flight response, 91
flow, 66, 69
focus, 61, 68–69, 72
Follett, Mary Parker, 4

forgetting, 80, 83
friction, avoiding, 93
future events, stress related to, 45–46

G

Galton, Francis, 11
generalized anxiety disorder, 52
generational communication barriers, 80–82
Generation X, 81
Generation Y, 81
Gen Z, 81–82
goal-related conflict, 89
goal setting, 103–104
Goleman, Daniel, 4, 6, 12
The Good Fight (Davey), 93
good stress, 44–45
Graves, Jean, 4

H

happiness, 16, 55, 102
help, seeking, 55, 104–105
horizontal thinking, 23–24
humility, 28
humor, 55

I

immediate return environments, 50–51
individualism, 104
Industrial Revolution, 4
initiative, 9
inner signals, attuning to, 7
intelligence quotient (IQ), x, 11–12
intention, 80, 83
internal EI barriers, 21
interruptions, 66–67
intrinsic drives, 8–9, 58
IQ (intelligence quotient), x, 11–12

J

journaling, xii, 29

K

Keats, John, 26
Kegan, Robert, 22
Key Executive Leadership Programs, ix

L

Lahey, Lisa, 22
language use, 76, 85
leaders, 5, 12, 25, 27
leadership
    after promotion, vii–viii, x
    controlling style of, 4
    emotional intelligence in, viii–x
    listening and, 97
    strategic approaches to, viii, 15
learning, 30
Leroy, Sophie, 64
Let It Be (album), ix
Let Your Life Speak (Palmer), 18
life experience, views and, 21
listening, 9, 86, 96–99
list making, 55–57
love, ix

M

Maslow, Abraham, 4
Mayer, John, 4
meaning making, 22–23
media multitasking, 63, 66
meditation, 29
memory, multitasking and, 66
mental health, 25, 42
mental stress reaction, 54
mentorship, 97
metrics, 24, 28
microaggressions, 76
Millennials, 81
mind, stages of, 21–23

mindfulness, xii, 17
motivation, 8–9, 38
    benefits of understanding, 16
    in communication, 74, 86
    in conflicts, 99
    in delayed return environment, 51
    happiness and success from, 102
    for listening, 98
    mindfulness for understanding, 17
    and multitasking, 68, 70, 72
    and stress, 41, 58
    for TD professionals, 40
motivation-based conflict, 90
multitasking, 59–72
    appropriate circumstances
        for, 67–68
    avoiding, 68–69
    case example, 59
    impact of, 65–67
    productivity while, 61–65
    reasons for, 60–61
    scheduling to prevent, 69–71
    by TD professionals, 39
    in workplace, 59–60
mutual interests, 95

N

National Institute of Mental Health
    (NIMH), 45
needs, 96, 105–106
neural pathways, 23, 30
neurological capital, for multitasking, 66
NIMH (National Institute of Mental
    Health), 45
noble intent, 30
nonverbal communication, 77–78, 82–83
noticing, 83–85

O

open mindedness, 95
open time, on calendar, 70
operational proficiency, vii

opposition, avoiding, 93
optimism bias, 103
orders, giving, ix
organizational capability, 37f
organizational culture, 27, 74, 94, 96
organizations
    benefits of emotional intelligence for,
        15–17
    conflict in, 92, 94
    defined, 26
    EI barriers in, 26–27
    poor communication in, 74
    role of TD professionals in, xi–xii
    with strategic leadership
        approaches, viii, 15
overthinking, 51–53
ownership, of personal baggage, 95

P

Palmer, Parker, 18
passion, 8
past events and experiences, 46, 53, 91
patience, 85, 98
pattern recognition, 12
Payne, Wayne, 4
people, working with, 35–36
Perceived Stress Scale, 47
perception-based conflict, 89
perfectionism, 51
performance, 16, 42–43
perseverance, 9
personal capability, 37f
personal crucibles, 29–30
personality traits, 51–53
personal lives
    multitasking in, 59–60
    stress in, 49–50
physical communication barriers, 80
physical health, 14, 25, 43
physical reactions
    to conflict, 91
    to stress, 53
planning, in conflict management, 95

positional authority, ix
positive conflict, 94, 99–100
positive realism, 103–104
positivity, 9, 30, 55, 103
power-based conflict, 90
presentations, preparing for, 83
pressure-based conflict, 89–90
problem solving, listening vs., 98
productivity, multitasking and, 60–67
professional capability, 37f
proofreading, 83
public speaking, fear of, 79

R

Raz, Sivan, 4
realistic expectations, 54
realistic goals, 103–104
reality, managing your, 80, 85
recovery, 29
reflection, xii, 29–30, 38, 96
refocusing, after stress, 57
relationships
    avoiding conflict in, 91–92
    benefits of EI in, 14
    managing, 10–11
    positive conflict for building, 94
relaxation, 55
resilience, 9, 14, 29, 104
resource-based conflict, 89
response-ability, 8
role-based conflict, 89
role models, 36–38, 97
routine stress, 46
routine tasks, multitasking during, 67

S

Salovey, Peter, 4
Satipatthana Sutta, 17
schedules, 69–71
the self, 13–15, 24
self-assessment, 7
self-authoring mind, 22

self-awareness, 6–7
  for communication, 73–74, 86
  in conflicts, 88, 94, 99
  and goal setting, 104
  happiness and success from, 102
  individual benefits of increasing, 13–14
  mindfulness to increase, 17
  and multitasking, 60, 68, 70, 71
  and noticing, 83–84
  and stress, 41, 56, 57
  for TD professionals, 40
  and vulnerability, 28
self-care, 18–19, 104
selfishness, 18, 35
self-regulation, 7–8
  benefits of, 14
  in communication, 73–74, 86
  in conflicts, 94, 99
  happiness and success from, 102
  for listening, 97
  mindfulness to improve, 17
  and multitasking, 60, 68–69, 72
  self-awareness and, 7
  and stress, 41, 57
  for TD professionals, 40
self-sufficiency, 96, 104–105
self-transforming mind, 23
sick days, 16, 27, 43
Simon-Binet IQ test, 11, 12
"single tasking," 69
sleep problems, 65
social intelligence, 4
socialized mind, 22
social skills, 10–11
  for communication, 74, 86
  in conflicts, 99
  happiness and success from, 102
  mindfulness to improve, 17
  and multitasking, 72
  self-awareness and, 7
  and stress, 58
  for TD professionals, 40
soft skills, x–xi, 3, 28

software trackers, email, 69
strangers, conflict with, 87–88
strategic management approaches, vii–viii
Strayer, David, 68
stress, 41–58
  case example, 41
  categories of, 44–47
  defined, 44
  directly addressing cause of, 55–57
  EQ and, 14
  frequency of, 47–50
  and immediate vs. delayed return environments, 50–51
  personality traits contributing to, 51–53
  for TD professionals, 39
  in workplace, 41–44
stress management, 54–55
stress reactions, 53–54
style-based conflict, 90
subconscious EI barriers, 21
success, defining, 106–107
sudden stress, 46–47
supertaskers, 68, 71
support systems, building, 104–106
"Survey of American Fears," 25
sympathy, 10
systems approach, to organizations, 26

T
Talent Development Capability Model, 37, 37f
talent development (TD)
  professionals, 35–40
    benefits of EI for, x, 35–36
    change for, 52
    conflict for, 88–89
    organizational role of, xi–xii
    as role models, 36–38
    stumbling blocks for, 38–40
task-related conflict, 88–89
TD professionals. See talent development professionals

technical qualifications, x, 36, 101
technology, 30, 80
templates, written communication, 83
"The Discourse on the Establishing of
    Mindfulness," 27
thinking patterns, 23–24, 51
time management, 65
timers, 68–69
Tobias, Bob, 105
to-do lists, 55, 70–71
tone of voice, 76–77, 83
toxic organizational culture, 27, 46
tracking your success, 106–107
Traditionalists, 81, 82
traumatic stress, 47
trust, 3, 27, 96
turnover
    communication problems and, 74
    conflict as cause of, 92
    EI and reduction in, 16
    at organizations with toxic
        culture, 27
    stress and, 42, 43
2020 *Stress in America* report (APA), 42

U

uncertainty, 26, 92
University of Utah, 68
unknown, fear of, 25–26, 28
unresolved conflict, 92, 93
U.S. Navy, ix, 106

V

value, 22, 24
verbal communication, 76–78, 85
video recording, of presentation
    rehearsal, 83
vulnerability, 28–29, 38, 105

W

Watson, Jason, 68
wellness resources, 54
workday length, 41–42
"working through others" concept, 4
work insecurity, 43
work-life balance, 81
workplace
    avoiding conflict in, 91
    communication in, 73–76
    horizontal thinking in, 24
    impact of stress in, 41–44
    multitasking in, 59–60
    unresolved conflict in, 92
worry, 52
written communication, 78–79, 83, 85

Z

Zauderer, Don, ix
Zoom, 60, 77
Zysberg, Leehu, 4

About the Author

Patrick Malone is director of Key Executive Leadership Programs at American University in Washington, DC. He is a frequent guest lecturer on leadership and organizational dynamics and has extensive experience working with government leaders. Patrick's research, teaching, and scholarship include work in public sector leadership, executive problem solving, organizational analysis, ethics, and public administration and policy. He is a retired US Navy captain, having spent 22 years in a number of senior leadership and policy roles.